# Parlez-vous Français?

THANKS TO THE LIVING LANGUAGE TEAM: Tom Russell, Elizabeth Bennett, Christopher Warnasch, Zviezdana Verzich, Suzanne McQuade, Amelia Muqaddam, Denise De Gennaro, Linda Schmidt, John Whitman, Helen Kilcullen, Arlene Aizer, Heather Lanigan, and Sophie Chin.

Published in the United States by Living Language, A Random House Company.

www.livinglanguage.com

Editor: Christopher Warnasch
Production Editor: John Whitman
Production Managers: Helen Kilcullen and Heather Lanigan
Interior Design: Sophie Ye Chin

First Edition

ISBN 1-4000-2093-X

Library of Congress Cataloging-in-Publication Data available upon request.

This book is available for special discounts for bulk purchases for sales promotions or premiums. Special editions, including personalized covers, excerpts of existing books, and corporate imprints, can be created in large quantities for special needs. For more information, write to Special Markets/Premium Sales, 1745 Broadway, MD 6-2, New York, New York 10019 or e-mail specialmarkets@randomhouse.com.

PRINTED IN THE UNITED STATES OF AMERICA

10 9 8 7 6 5 4 3 2 1

# *Parlez-vous. Français?*

## LEARN FRENCH

### The Basics

by

**Jenny Barriol**

edited by

**Christopher A. Warnasch**

# Table of Contents

# *Introduction*

Welcome to *Parlez-vous français ? Learn French: The Basics,* an exciting and entertaining new way to learn French, brought to you by LIVING LANGUAGE and THE STANDARD DEVIANTS.

This is the right course for you if A) you've always wanted to learn French, B) you've never had the time, and C) you've been bored to tears or scared senseless by more traditional courses. The experts at Living Language and The Standard Deviants have gotten together to bring you something truly unique – a course that's fun and entertaining, complete with a perfectly coordinated book and DVD that really, honestly work. This is the perfect way to learn French for anyone who wants to have a good time along with all the learning. Maybe you're going on a trip to Paris, or you want to impress someone special, or you want to get ahead on the job, or you're just looking for some personal enrichment. Or maybe you're taking an introductory French course but need a little extra inspiration to make sense of it all. In any of those cases, this is a great course for you.

Here's how it works. The package includes a 192-page book and a DVD, each of which is the perfect companion to the other. The book and the DVD work together to teach and reinforce, and to give you plenty of opportunity to learn, practice, and review. They're simple to use. The course has five parts, and each of those parts is divided into a few sections. All you have to do is read a section in the book, complete with explanations, examples, vocabulary and practice exercises. Then, once you're finished digesting the information, watch the corresponding section on the DVD. You'll find more explanations, more examples, and even more practice exercises. And last, for good measure, turn back to the book and do the review exercises. Simple! Here goes again:

1. Start with the book. Read the section, learn the vocabulary, and do the Practice Exercises.
2. Watch the corresponding section on the DVD. First choose "Select Lesson" on the main menu, and then choose the appropriate part, 1, 2, 3, 4, or 5. Then advance to the right section.
3. Turn back to the book. Do the Review Exercises at the end of the section to wrap it all up.

This course covers all of the basics of French. You'll learn correct pronunciation, greetings and basic vocabulary, how to talk a little bit about yourself and ask about others, and you'll get a good taste of grammar. This is the perfect way to start learning French – you'll get a solid foundation in what you absolutely need to know, and best of all, you'll actually *enjoy* doing it, so you'll be all set to continue your studies! Great, right?

Ready? Let's begin.

## *How to Use the DVD*

1. Place the **DVD** disk into the player. After a brief intro, the main menu will appear on the screen.

2. Use the **UP** and **DOWN** arrows to move among the menu choices. Press **ENTER** to select.

3. During the program, press **MENU** to return to the main menu. Access special features, including **HELPFUL INFO** and the **FINAL EXAM** from the main menu.

4. During the program, press the **NEXT** and **PREV** buttons to skip through major sections of the program.

# Au Début

PART

# Before We Get Started

In Part 1, *Au Début* or "In the Beginning," you're going to learn how to pronounce French correctly. We'll cover it all – the alphabet, vowels, consonants, that crazy French way of spelling words, all of those accents . . . In fact, you're just a few pages away from knowing how to pronounce French. Wow. But before we get started, here are a few thoughts to make this as easy as possible.

First of all, know that you know more than you know . . . Um, wait . . . , let's rephrase that. Let's say that you already know much more French than you think . . . Really? Yes! Take a look at this: "introduction" in English, "*introduction*" *en français*. You see? You had no problem understanding that! There are a lot of similar words between French and English. These words are called "cognates." The main reason for this similarity is that *le français* is a Romance language, a language derived from Latin (which was spoken in Rome and the Roman Empire, so, "romance."). Believe or not, about half of the English language has its roots there, too. So English and French do have a lot in common.

Now, why do you want to learn French? Because you have no choice? Is it part of your school curriculum? Oh, well. Or because you love those French movies? Or, because it's a cool way to impress your friends? Well, whatever your motivation may be, it is indeed a good thing to learn at least one foreign language, as it broadens and widens and stretches your mind and imagination. And you made a good choice with French! You see, a long time ago, French was the international language. And, although that is no longer the case, French is still spoken in . . . France, of course, as well as in Canada, in several countries in Africa such as Senegal, Guinea, Congo, Côte d'Ivoire, Burkina Faso; in Guadeloupe, Martinique, and Haiti in the Caribbean; and also by many people in the Middle East and other regions of the world. Plus, there's all of that great wine and food, fantastic literature, history, film, fashion . . .

And why this course? For one thing, it uses the "functional approach", which is thought to be the best way to teach and learn French (and any other language). This approach constantly invites the student to communicate and get by in the foreign language. Plus, it's fun and practical. In short, this course was designed to be a simple, entertaining and effective way to get your feet wet in French!

Are you feeling better? . . . Good! Because you won't be learning just words, but phrases, idioms and full sentences, as well as basic grammar. And you will have lots of opportunities to PRACTICE all through this course. Yes, practice is the key! Ready to go?

*Bienvenue* ! Welcome!

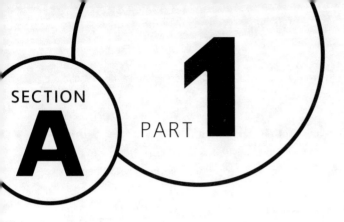

## *The Alphabet*

As we've said before, there are a lot of similarities between English and French: a common alphabet, in most cases, the same sentence construction, and similar words... So, you may wonder, "what's the catch?" *La prononciation*, pronunciation, but of course! French pronunciation can be... how to put it... well, weird! When learning it, you will need to use everything in your mouth: the top of your throat, the sides and top of your mouth, your tongue, your teeth, your lips and even your nose. *Bizarre*, as they say...

But before we get to the alphabet, let's collect some words. We'll start each section by giving you some new words you'll come across in that section. In this case, the words will be examples of different things you need to know about pronunciation. Look at the list of words, say them aloud (with the help of the phonetics provided!), write them down a few times if you'd like. The idea is for you to be able to recognize them as you read through the section in the book and then watch it on the DVD. Soon enough you'll have memorized all of this new vocabulary. And you'll recognize some French words that are cognates, so those will be easy to remember, like "free-bee's."

There are many TIPS for learning vocabulary: repetition of the word (like twenty times!), flash cards with the English word on one side and its equivalent in French on the other, "self quizzes", labeling things, finding memory tricks, having index cards with groups of words on particular subjects, etc. But don't feel pressured to memorize the whole vocabulary list each time you see it at the start of a section. Work with it – it'll come slowly, and that's just fine.

And one more helpful hint . . . When learning a French noun, make it a habit to memorize both the noun and its corresponding article. That is "the" and "a" in English, and *le, la, un,* or *une* in French. It's just an extra syllable to learn, but it'll make your life easier later on.

## POINT 1: VOCABULARY

These are the words that you'll see in Part 1, Section A. In Part 1, which deals with pronunciation, you'll see the phonetic [fuh-NEH-tik] transcription of each word. This strange looking code is meant to help you until you learn how to pronounce these words on your own. Think of the phonetics as training wheels. They're a bit wobbly and imperfect, but they'll keep you going until you can go it alone. The only thing that might throw you at first is when you see something like this: *bon* [BOH*n.] Don't worry; that asterisk just means that the vowel is nasal. We'll cover that in just a little bit. (Plus, you'll hear all of these words on the DVD, anyway!)

*la, le, l'* [LAH, LUH] – the (singular)
*une, un* [EWN, UH*n] – a, an
*oui* [WEE] – yes
*non* [NOH*n] – no
*et* [EH] – and
*ou* [OO] – or
*le français* [luh frah*n-SEH] – French (language), a French man
*la prononciation* [lah proh-noh*n-syah-SYOH*n] – pronunciation

**une introduction** [ewn eh*n-troh-dewk-SYOH*n] – introduction

**bienvenue** [byeh*n-vuh-NEW] – welcome

**bonjour** [boh*n-ZHOOR] – hello

**au revoir** [oh ruh-VWAHR] – goodbye

**salut** [sah-LEW] – hello /goodbye (colloquial)

**je m'appelle . . .** [zhuh mah-PEHL] – my name is . . .

**à** [AH] – in / to / at

**où** [OO] – where

**le chat** [luh SHAH] – the cat

**le chien** [luh SHYEH*n] – the dog

**la fille** [lah FEE-yuh] – the girl / the daughter

**un homme** [uh NUHM] – a man

**une femme** [ewn FAHM] – a woman

**le café** [luh kah-FEH] – coffee, café, coffeeshop

**le thé** [luh TAY] – tea

**la photographie** [lah foh-toh-grah-FEE] – photography

**avoir** [ah-VWAHR] – to have

**brune** [BREWN] (feminine) – of a brownish color / with brown hair

**brun** [BRUH*n] (masculine) – of a brownish color / with brown hair

**qu'est-ce que tu dis ?** [KEHS-kuh tew DEE] – what are you saying? (informal)

**tu penses** [tew PAH*nS] – you think

**que** [KUH] – that

**a l'air** [ah LEHR] – looks, seems

**bizarre** [bee-ZAHR] – weird

**répétez !** [ray-pay-TAY] – repeatl

**merci** [mehr-SEE] – thank you

**s'il vous plaît** [see(l)-voo-PLEH] – please

**un fiancé** [uh*n fyah*n-SAY] – a fiancé (masculine)

**une fiancée** [ewn fyah*n-SAY] – a fiancée (feminine)

**blanc, blanche** [BLAH*n, BLAH*nSH] – white (masculine / feminine)

**jaune** [ZHOHN] – yellow (masculine / feminine)

**vert, verte** [VEHR, VEHRT] – green (masculine / feminine)

*noir, noire* [NWAHR] – black (masculine / feminine)

*Genève* [zhuh-NEHV] – Geneva

**PRACTICE EXERCISE 1**

Let's put some of that to practice. Answer each of the following questions.

1. Write the three ways of translating "the" singular _____ _____
   _____.

2. Now write the two ways of saying "a" or "an" _____ _____.

3. Write "hello" _____

4. Now write "goodbyel" _____

5. Write "thank you" _____

6. Now write "please" _____

7. Write "a woman" _____

8. Now write "a man" _____

9. A banana's color is _____.

10. When you want to tell someone your name, you say: _____.

**PRACTICE EXERCISE 2**

Match each English word in the left column with the French word in the right column.

1. *oui*            welcome
2. *le chat*        the coffee
3. *le chien*       yes
4. *la fille*       to have
5. *le café*        the cat
6. *noir*           the girl
7. *bienvenue*      the dog
8. *avoir*          black

## POINT 2: THE ALPHABET

Remember French and English share (pretty much) the same alphabet, but with a few different pronunciations. Here are the 26 letters:

*a, b, c, d, e, f, g, h, i, j, k, l, m, n, o, p, q, r, s, t, u, v, w, x, y, z.*

And this is the way these letters are pronounced:

*ah, bay, say, day, uh, ehf, zhay, ahsh, ee, zhee, kah, ehl, ehm, ehn, oh, peh, kew, ehr, ehs, tay, ew, vay, doo-bluh vay, eeks, ee-grehk, zehd*

There are a few letters to pay special attention to. "E" is called *uh* in French, and "G" is *zhay*, while "J" is *zhee*. "Q" [*kew*] and "U" [*ew*] share a vowel that we're writing for now as *ew*, but it sounds like the *ü* in German, if you know what that sounds like. If you don't, no problem – we'll come back to it and tell you all about it. "W" is called a double V in French, a *doo-bluh vay*. And "Y" is a "Greek I," or an *ee-grehk*.

*TIP:* When watching someone speak French, focus on their mouth. See how they grin. It may seem goofy, but don't forget your purpose. You have to come up with the same sounds. If you can, copy their way of speaking in front of a mirror and don't be afraid to exaggerate!

### PRACTICE EXERCISE 3

Write the French names for each of these letters.

1. A
2. W
3. G
4. I
5. E
6. S
7. B
8. Z
9. J
10. Q

## POINT 3: THE CONSONANTS

French consonants are for the most part similar to English consonants. But there are a few that can be tricky. Watch out for these consonants:

**C**   can be pronounced K, as in "carrot" or "cape", in front of *a, o, u.*
*le café* [luh kah-FEH].
Or it can be pronounced S, as in "circle", in front of: *e, i, y.*
*merci* [mehr-SEE], *la fiancée* [lah fyah\*n-SAY]

**CH**   *C* with an *H* is pronounced SH, as in "shine".
*le chat* [luh SHAH]

**G**   can be pronounced as a hard G, as in "guy" in front of: *a, o, u, l, r.*
*le garage* [luh gah-RAHZH] – the first G, at least.
Or, it can be pronounced ZH, as in "pleasure" in front of: *e, i, y.*
*Genève* [zhay-NEHV] – or the second G in *garage* [gah-RAHZH]

**GN**   is pronounced NY as in "onion" or "canyon".
*le cygne* [luh SEE-nyuh]

**H**   is silent, as in "hour" or the American pronunciation of "herb."
*l'hôtel* [loh-TEHL]
Or, sometimes, it's called "*h aspiré*", which means it's still silent, but it keeps you from linking sounds, which you'll learn how to do soon!
*le haricot* [luh ah-ree-KOHT] (Instead of *l'haricot*. Don't worry. You'll see more on this later.)

With other consonants, *h* has no effect on the pronunciation, except, as we just mentioned, after a *c* [*CH*], and right after a *p* [PH], which sounds like "F," just like in English.
*le chat* [luh SHAH] , *la photo* [lah foh-TOH]

**LL**   preceded by *i*, two *L*'s are pronounced YUH as in "yup".
*la fille* [lah FEE-yuh]

**Q**   is called *kew*, with the very French sharp *U* (say "ee" with plucked lipsl). You'll always see it followed by the letter *u* then an other vowel, and it is pronounced like a K.
*que* [KUH]

**R**   is harder and throatier than in English. Quite a guttural sound from the back of your mouth, a bit like a garglel *rouge* [ROOZH]

**S**   at the beginning of a word or followed by another *S* or a consonant is pronounced as in "salt."
*le soleil* [luh soh-LAY]
Or, between two vowels, it is pronounced Z, like in "rose"
*la rose* [lah ROHZ]

**T**   followed by an *h* is pronounced just like a regular T. Nothing like our English TH . . .
*le thé* [luh TAY]

Final consonants are generally silent in French, except for the consonants in the word CaReFuL. So, these words all end in silent consonants: *vas, nous, oiseaux, français, beaucoup, intéressant, bientôt, cas, avez*. But these words end in pronounced final "CaReFuL" consonants: *avec, parc, bonjour, revoir, neuf, chef, il, seul*. The ending *–er* is an exception to the CaReFuL rule; that *–r* is silent, and the ending sounds a bit like "-ay." *Chanter* is [shah*n-TAY] for example.

**PRACTICE EXERCISE 4**

Choose the best phonetic transcription for each of the following words. Here's a hint – check out the pronunciation of those tricky consonants!

1. *le chat* – [luh KAH] or [luh SHAH]
2. *le thé* – [luh TAY] or [luh THAY]
3. *l'hôtel* – [loh-TEHL] or [luh hoh-TEHL]
4. *le cygne* – [luh SEEG-nuh] or [luh SEE-nyuh]
5. *le garage* – [luh gah-RAHZH] or [luh zhah-RAHZH]
6. *la rose* – [lah ROHSS] or [lah ROHZ]

Remember to choose "Select Lesson" on the main menu, and then "Part 1."

( **WATCH THE DVD** )

Great! Now it's time for you to turn on your DVD and watch Part 1, Section A. This stuff will all be second nature! Then come back to the book, and be ready for a review of the whole thing.

# *REVIEW EXERCISES*

Now that you've read about Part 1, Section A, and seen it on the DVD as well, here's a chance to show what you know.

**REVIEW EXERCISE 1**

Translate each of the following words or phrases into English.

1. *le chat*
2. *salut*
3. *la fille*
4. *un homme*
5. *Je m'appelle Véronique.*
6. *Qu'est-ce que tu dis ?*

**REVIEW EXERCISE 2**

Now translate each of the following words into French.

1. photography
2. weird
3. please
4. the tea
5. goodbye
6. welcome

**REVIEW EXERCISE 3**

Find one word starting with each of the following letters or letter combinations. You can go back and look at your list of vocabulary if you need to!

1. *c:*
2. *ch:*
3. *h* (mute):
4. *h* (*aspiré*):
5. *ph:*
6. *th:*
7. *q:*
8. *f:*

**REVIEW EXERCISE 4**

True or False? (*Vrai ou Faux ?*)

1. V   F   The combination *ch* is pronounced like the "c" in "cat."
2. V   F   The French *th* and the English "th" are pronounced the same.
3. V   F   The French and the English alphabets are completely different.
4. V   F   *Photo* in French is pronounced the same as "photo" in English.
5. V   F   The French *c* has more than one pronunciation.
6. V   F   The French *s* is always pronounced the same way.
7. V   F   In French, *brun* is a color.
8. V   F   French and English have nothing in common.

# Answer Key

## PRACTICE EXERCISE 1

**1.** le, la, l' **2.** un, une **3.** bonjour ! or salut ! **4.** au revoir ! or salut ! **5.** merci
**6.** s'il vous plaît **7.** une femme **8.** un homme **9.** jaune **10.** je m'appelle . . .

## PRACTICE EXERCISE 2

**1.** oui – yes **2.** le chat – the cat **3.** le chien – the dog **4.** la fille – the girl **5.** le
café – the coffee **6.** noir – black **7.** bienvenue – welcome **8.** avoir – to have

## PRACTICE EXERCISE 3

**1.** ah **2.** doo-bluh vay **3.** zhay **4.** ee **5.** uh **6.** ehs **7.** bay **8.** zehd **9.** zhee
**10.** kew

## PRACTICE EXERCISE 4

**1.** luh SHAH **2.** luh TAY **3.** loh-TEHL **4.** luh SEE-nyuh **5.** luh gah-RAHZH **6.** lah
ROHZ

## REVIEW EXERCISE 1

**1.** the cat **2.** hi, or bye **3.** the girl **4.** a man **5.** My name is Véronique. **6.** What
are you saying?

## REVIEW EXERCISE 2

**1.** la photographie **2.** bizarre **3.** s'il vous plaît **4.** le thé **5.** au revoir
**6.** bienvenue

## REVIEW EXERCISE 3

Some possible answers are:
**1.** cygne, café **2.** chat, chien **3.** hôtel, homme **4.** haricot **5.** photographie,
photo **6.** thé **7.** que **8.** français, femme, fiancé, fiancée,

**REVIEW EXERCISE 4**

**1.** faux: It's pronounced like the "sh" in "shoe." **2.** faux: A French th is pronounced like an English "t." **3.** faux: They have many similarities. **4.** vrai **5.** vrai **6.** faux: It can be pronounced like the "ss" in "hiss" or the "s" in "rose." **7.** vrai **8.** faux: They share a lot of cognates.

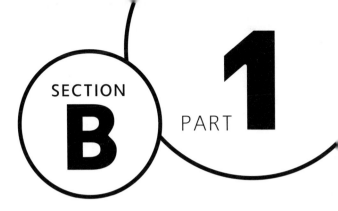

# VOWELS & ACCENTS

Now let's move on to vowels and accent marks, which are the most difficult thing about French pronunciation really. But before we do that, let's add some words to your vocabulary. Remember that the key is to get you familiar with these words so that you'll recognize them later in the lesson and on the DVD. Ready?

### POINT 1: VOCABULARY

*lui* [LWEE] – him

*elle* [EHL] – her

*le vœu* [luh VUH] – the wish

*vain* [VEH*n] – vain

*loin* [LWEH*n] – far

*le cygne* [luh SEE-nyuh] – the swan

*le père* [luh PEHR] – the father

*la mère* [lah MEHR] – the mother

*un élève* [uh nay-LEV] – a (male) student

*une élève* [ewn ay-LEV] – a (female) student

*l'eau* [LOH] – water

*le garçon* [luh gahr-SOH*n] – the boy

*Noël* [noh-WEHL] – Christmas

*la lune* [lah LEWN] – the moon

*le soleil* [luh soh-LAY] – the sun

*un hôtel* [uh noh-TEHL] – a hotel

*être* [EH-truh] – to be

*une rose* [ewn ROHZ] – a rose

*rose* [ROHZ] – pink

*rouge* [ROOZH] – red

**PRACTICE EXERCISE 1**

Connect the French words on the left with their English meanings on the right.

| | | |
|---|---|---|
| 1. | *une rose* | the swan |
| 2. | *le garçon* | the mother |
| 3. | *le cygne* | she, her |
| 4. | *lui* | the boy |
| 5. | *le soleil* | a (male) student |
| 6. | *la mère* | a rose |
| 7. | *elle* | far |
| 8. | *une élève* | a (female) student |
| 9. | *un élève* | the sun |
| 10. | *loin* | him |

## POINT 2: THE VOWELS

Once again, the vowels in French are *a, e, i, o, u,* and *y*. That looks familiar, right? And don't forget their names: *ah, uh, ee, oh, ew,* and *ee-grehk*. Keep in mind that in French, vowel sounds are short, pure, and steady. What that means is that French vowels have one sound – *o* is just "oh," not the "oh-woo" of our drawn-out English "o". And *é* is just "ay" – not "ay-yee" as in English.

The simple vowels are pronounced just like their names – *ah, uh, ee, oh,* and *ew,* and *ee-grehk* is pronounced just like *ee*. As long as you remember to keep the sounds pure and crisp, the only vowel that might give you a problem is *u*. That's the one that sounds like a German *ü*. And if you don't know German, than just try this: start to say "ee." Hold it – "ee-ee-ee-ee-ee-ee-ee . . . " Now, while you're still saying "ee," change the shape of your lips so that they look like a trumpet, as if you're puckering up to plant a big kiss on someone's cheek. Everything else is still saying "ee," but the shape of your lips will change the sound into a perfect French *u*. (Remember that for now, we're showing that sound as "ew" but that's just a symbol we're using.)

Try saying these words to hear the sound of each vowel.

**A**   *la* [LAH]

**E**   *le* [LUH]

**I**   *merci* [mehr-SEE]

**O**   *soleil* [soh-LAY]

**U**   *lune* [LEWN] (Round those lips!)

**Y**   *cygne* [SEE-nyuh]

**POINT 3:** THE ACCENTS & OTHER SIGNS

French has more accents than you would probably hope! But don't worry; they're really not that hard. Let's start by giving them names and seeing some examples of them. (You'll also get some silly devices to help you remember their names!)

` is called *l'accent grave* [lahk-sah\*n GRAHV]. It slopes up backwards, like someone falling into a "grave." You can see it in: *le père* [luh PEHR].

´ is called *l'accent aigu* [lahk-sah\*n teh-GEW]. *Aigu* means "sharp," like a sword, and if you look at the accent mark, you see that it slopes up and forward, like a sword ready for battle. You can see it on the first *e* in the word *l'élève* [lay-LEHV].

ˆ is called *l'accent circonflexe* [lahk-sah\*n seer-koh\*n-FLEX.] It looks like a hat, or maybe a bicep being "flexed." You can see it in *l'hôtel*. [loh-TEHL]

And there are two other signs you should be able to recognize.

**ç** is called *la cédille* [lah say-DEE-yuh]; it's that little tail on a *C*. You can see it in *le garçon* [luh gahr-SOHn].

¨ is *le tréma* [luh tray-MAH]. It's the pair of dots over a vowel that looks a bit German. It's only in a few words in French, such as *Noël* [noh-WEHL].

Now that we know what the accents are called, let's see how they work. All in all, an accent usually serves to change the pronunciation of a vowel, or show a difference between two words that would otherwise be spelled exactly alike. Let's take them one accent at a time.

1.  You'll find the *accent grave* on:

    è                          *la mère* [lah MEHR]

    The accent affects the sound of the letter *e*; the EH sound becomes very open, as in "said" or "bet". You'll also see it on:

    à                          *à* [AH]

    ù                          *où* [OO]

    Good news! The *accent grave* on *a* or *u* doesn't change the sound. But it does distinguish the words from potential look-alikes. For example, *a* means "has" but *à* means "to" or "at." And *ou* means "or" but *où* means "where."

2.  The *accent aigu* is found on:

    é                          *l'élève* [lay-LEHV]

    The accent affects the sound of the letter *e* again. But here *e* sounds slightly open, as in "day" or "bake".

3.  The *accent circonflexe* is found on:

    ê                          *être* [EH-truh]

    The accent affects the sound of the letter *e* the same way than the *accent grave*; the EH sound becomes very open, as in "said" or "bet". And here is more good news! On the other letters: *a, o, u, i*, the *accent circonflexe* doesn't change the sound at all.

*TIP:* You'll often see this accent over a letter that used to have a *s* after it in Latin. But since we've got some Latin in our language too, you'll recognize this. For instance, *hôtel* looks a lot like "hostel", right? And what about *hôpital* and *forêt*? What do you get if you add the "s" back in?

4. *La cédille* is used with the letter *c*:

   ç                              *le français* [luh frah*n-SEH] or *le garçon* [luh gahr-
                                  SOH*n]

   You'll only find it on *c* in front of *a, o, u*. If you think back to the last section, you know that a *c* before *a, o,* or *u* is pronounced like a K. But not if there's a *cédille* on it! Then it sounds just like an "s".

5. Finally, there's *le tréma* (two dots, or dieresis), which is used to separate the sounds of two vowels that are next to each other.

   ë                              *Noël* [noh-EHL]

**PRACTICE EXERCISE 2**

True or False? (*Vrai ou Faux ?*)

1.    V    F    The vowels *é* and *è* are pronounced the same.
2.    V    F    Accent marks always change pronunciation.
3.    V    F    The *cédille* makes a *c* sound like an *s*.
4.    V    F    The letter *è* sounds like "eh."
5.    V    F    The two dots over a vowel are called a *circonflexe*.

**POINT 4:** THE DIPHTHONGS

Diphthongs are pairs or groups of vowels that create one sound. They're like a duet or trio of vowels playing together, instead of one vowel giving a solo performance. English is full of diphthongs: "cow", "say", "boat", "toy" etc … If you say "cow" really slowly, you'll hear that the vowel is actually a combination of the "ah" and "oh" sounds, with some other stuff thrown in,

like an "oo.". And "say" is really something like "seh" followed by "ee."
Those are diphthongs!

French has its fair share of diphthongs as well. And here they are for your
pronouncing enjoyment.

| | |
|---|---|
| *ai* | has the same pronunciation as *é*. Kind of between "eh" and "ay." |
| | *le français* [luh frah*n-SEH] |
| *au* | has the same pronunciation as the letter *o*. |
| | *l'eau* [LOH] |
| *ei* | has the same pronunciation as *é*. But before the letter *l*, *ei* sounds like *è*. |
| | *le soleil* [luh soh-LEH] |
| *eu* | has the same pronunciation as the letter *e*, like the u in "put" but tighter. Like a rounded "oo" in "took." |
| | *bleu* [BLUH] |
| *oi* | is pronounced a bit like WAH. |
| | *au revoir* [oh ruh-VWAHR] |
| *œ* | has the same pronunciation as the letter *e*. |
| | *le vœu* [luh VUH] |
| *ou* | is pronounced OO like in "pool". Don't forget that *u* alone is that pucker sound. |
| | *rouge* [ROOZH] |
| *ui* | is pronounced a bit like WEE. But the first part of the sound is the puckered *u*. |
| | *lui* [LEWEE] |
| *oui* | is pronounced like OOWEE. The first part of the sound is OO, and then EE. |
| | *oui* [WEE] |

In French you'll also see a lot of vowels or vowel combinations followed by an –n or an –m. These are called "nasal vowels" – don't be afraid to use your nose to pronounce them! And don't think that they're so foreign – you'll also find plenty of this in English, but we tend not to make a big deal of them. Say "sing" out loud. Now say it again, but this time hold your nose, like you've just smelled something awful. Do you hear how different the nose-held "sing" sounds? That's because a lot of the sound (air) is passing through your nose when you say "sing." And if you block your nose, the air can't do what it normally does, so the sound changes.

In each of the following French sounds, a lot of air has to pass through your nose. You don't even actually pronounce the –n or the –m. It's just there as a signal that a lot of the vowel should go through your nose instead of your mouth. And, by the way, that's what all of this asterisk business in the phonetics has been about. Have you noticed that? Did you guess that the asterisk in *bon* [BOH*n] meant a nasal vowel? Let's look at them all now.

| | |
|---|---|
| *an / am /* *en / em* | are pronounced a bit like the English word "on", but the air goes through the nose. *français* [frah*n-SEH] |
| *ain / aim /* *ein / eim* | are all pronounced like the English "end" with the "–d" sound cut off. Imagine that you're saying "eh?" because you haven't heard what someone said to you. *vain* [VEH*n] |
| *un / um* | are also pronounced a bit like "end" . . . only the lips are more open. Think about what you say when you're searching for a word: "He's just so . . . he's so . . . what's the word I'm looking for . . . uhhhh . . ." *un* [EH*n] |

| *oin / oim* | are pronounced a bit like "when" with the –n cut off. The sound is actually close to the way you'd imitate a crying baby: "wha . . . wha . . . " |
| | *loin* [LWEH*n] |
| *on / om* | are pronounced like . . . , well like . . . you know . . . [OH*n]. It's pretty close to the vowel in "don't" – just cut off the d– and the –t, make your lips round, say "oh", but let that beautiful sound come out through your nose! |
| | *non* [NOH*n] |

And there's one peculiar case: *-em* is pronounced AM as in "Sam" in the word *femme* (woman). Even though it looks like it should be nasal, it's not!

## PRACTICE EXERCISE 3

Which words rhyme with . . .

1. *et:*        *français – au revoir – s'il vous plaît – un fiancé*
2. *la:*        *à – hôtel – air – chat*
3. *merci:*     *répétez – photographie – bleu – que*
4. *le:*        *bleu – jaune – que – café*
5. *lune:*      *cygne – thé – une – rose*
6. *eau:*       *auto – garçon – blanc – le*

**( WATCH THE DVD )**

And now, back to your favorite DVD! "Select Lesson," then "Part 1," and then advance to section B. Then come back for more!

# REVIEW EXERCISES

### REVIEW EXERCISE 1

Can you guess what these phrases mean? You've seen the individual words before, but now try to put them together.

1. *Répétez,*
   *s'il vous-plaît!*
2. *le chat noir*
3. *le chien bizarre*
4. *le garçon et la fille*
5. *l'hôtel blanc*
6. *Qu'est-ce que tu dis ?*
7. *la rose rose*
8. *le cygne bleu*
9. *la femme et l'homme*
10. *un chien rouge*

### REVIEW EXERCISE 2

Write down whether each of the following words has a nasal vowel or not.

1. *bon*
2. *homme*
3. *chien*
4. *accent*
5. *femme*
6. *mère*
7. *hôtel*
8. *loin*

### REVIEW EXERCISE 3

Missing Accents! Some of the following words are missing accents. Rewrite the ones that don't have their correct accents.

1. *hopital*
2. *pere*
3. *chat*
4. *l'eau*
5. *etre*
6. *garcon*

# Answer Key

## PRACTICE EXERCISE 1

**1.** une rose – a rose **2.** le garçon – the boy **3.** le cygne – the swan **4.** lui – him
**5.** le soleil – the sun **6.** la mère – the mother **7.** elle – she **8.** une élève – a
(female) student **9.** un élève – a (male) student **10.** loin – far

## PRACTICE EXERCISE 2

**1.** faux: Roughly, é is like "ay" and è is like "eh." **2.** faux: Sometimes accents
do not affect pronunciation. **3.** vrai **4.** vrai **5.** faux: The two dots are called a
tréma.

## PRACTICE EXERCISE 3

**1.** français, s'il vous plaît, un fiancé **2.** à, chat **3.** photographie **4.** bleu, que
**5.** Une **6.** auto

## REVIEW EXERCISE 1

**1.** Repeat, please! **2.** the black cat **3.** the strange/weird dog **4.** the boy and
the girl **5.** the white hotel **6.** What are you saying? **7.** the pink rose **8.** the
blue swan **9.** the woman and the man **10.** a red dog

## REVIEW EXERCISE 2

**1.** nasal **2.** not nasal **3.** nasal **4.** nasal **5.** not nasal **6.** not nasal **7.** not nasal
**8.** nasal

## REVIEW EXERCISE 3

**1.** hôpital **2.** père **3.** chat **4.** l'eau **5.** être **6.** garçon

# Mes Préférences

PART 2

## *Small Talk*

The name of Part 2 is *Mes Préférences*, or "My Preferences." Pretty obvious, huh? Again, it's all of those wonderful cognates that make English and French so similar. Except of course for the pronunciation, which you completely mastered in Part 1. So now you're eager to be able to express what you like and don't like, who you are, how you're doing, etc., right? Well, lucky you, that's exactly what you're going to learn in Part 2! But first it's time to pump up the *vocabulaire* . . .

> **POINT 1:** VOCABULARY

How are you doing on this so far? Finding it easy to remember those French words? Well, as you've seen before, there's nothing like PRACTICE! And don't forget that we've taken off the phonetic training wheels from now on.

| | |
|---|---|
| *je* | I |
| *tu, vous* | you |
| *nous* | we |
| *me* | me |
| *mon, ma, mes* | my |
| *ton, ta, tes* | your |
| *son, sa, ses* | his, her, its |

| | |
|---|---|
| *bonjour* | hello, good day |
| *salut* | hello, hi |
| *au revoir* | goodbye |
| *bonsoir* | good evening, hello, goodbye |
| *bien* | well |
| *mal* | bad, not well |
| *pas mal* | not bad, okay |
| *comment* | how |
| *madame* | Madam, Mrs., Ms. |
| *monsieur* | Mr., Sir |
| *mademoiselle* | Miss |
| *je m'appelle . . .* | my name is . . . |
| *Comment t'appelles -tu ?* | What's your name? |
| *présenter* | to introduce |
| *enchanté, enchantée* | pleased to meet you |
| *aller* | to go |
| *Comment vas-tu ?* | How are you? (familiar) |
| *Comment allez-vous ?* | How are you? (polite) |
| *Comment ça va ?* | How are you doing? |
| *Quoi de neuf ?* | What's up?, What's new? |
| *super* | super |
| *ok* | okay |
| *formidable* | great |
| *un ami, l'ami* | a friend, the friend (male) |
| *une amie, l'amie* | a friend, the friend (female) |
| *le pays* | the country |
| *les États-Unis* | The United States |
| *La France* | France |
| *la préférence* | the preference |

**PRACTICE EXERCISE 1**

Connect the French words on the left with their meanings on the right.

| | | |
|---|---|---|
| 1. | *enchanté(e)* | the friend |
| 2. | *aller* | hello |
| 3. | *comment* | we |
| 4. | *le pays* | great |
| 5. | *l'ami* | pleased to meet you |
| 6. | *nous* | The United States |
| 7. | *formidable* | how |
| 8. | *les États-Unis* | to go |
| 9. | *salut* | the country |
| 10. | *présenter* | to introduce |

## POINT 4: SAYING *BONJOUR*!

Of course, one of the most important things to know how to say is "Hello!" In French, just like in English, there are different things you can say, depending on the time of day and how familiar or polite you want to be. You don't say, "Hey! What up?" to a teacher or a boss, do you?

*Bonjour* is the most common greeting. It means "hello" or "hi" or "good day" and can be either formal or familiar. You can use it in the morning or the afternoon. When it gets more toward the evening, you should say *bonsoir*, which is "hello" or "good evening." *Bonsoir* can also be used when you're leaving, as a stand-in for *au revoir*, which means "goodbye." *Bonjour* can't be used to say "goodbye," though. (Goodbye is *au revoir*.)

A more informal greeting, like "hey!" or "hi!," is *salut*. You can use it with friends or family members, or anyone you're being chummy with. You could even say *ciao!*, which isn't very French, but then again it's not very English, either, and English speakers use it all the time.

To say "see you later" you can say *à plus tard*, and "see you soon" is *à bientôt*. *À la prochaine* means something like "until the next time," although it doesn't sound quite so odd in French. And finally, if you're turning in for the night, say *bonne nuit* ! But note that that's something you say when you're going to bed, not just when you're leaving someone's house in the evening after a dinner or a party. In those cases, you'd say *bonne soirée*, which is close to "enjoy the rest of your evening."

## POINT 3: *TU* OR *VOUS*?

In French, there are two forms of the subject pronoun "you," a formal or polite form, and a familiar form. The formal "you" is *vous* in both the singular and plural . It's used among adults who are not close, for examples among colleagues at work or people in any other formal situation. It's also used in situations where people do not know one another, such as in stores among salespeople and clients.

The familiar form of "you" is *tu* in the singular, and *vous* again in the plural. It's used within families and among friends and young people, and actually, more and more in work situations as formality gives way to familiarity. That means that you would call your friend *tu*, but if you're talking to two or three of your friends, you'd call them *vous*.

You may be wondering how you'd know when to adress an adult as *tu*. The easy answer is you'd know because you'd only do it when invited to! This might be something like calling a person Mr. or Mrs. So and So, only to have them say, "Please, call me John," or "Please call me Barbara." There's a special verb in French, *tutoyer*, which means "to call someone *tu*" instead of *vous*. So, a French person might say to you, *Et si on se tutoyait ?* which means something along the lines of "How about calling each other *tu*?" The fact is that *vous* used to be the norm, and it's begun to fade over the past years. Still, use *vous* when in doubt!

**PRACTICE EXERCISE 2**

Would you use *tu* or *vous*? Try your hand at the following situations.

1. If you're speaking to your teacher?
2. If you're speaking to your mother?
3. If you're speaking to your boss?
4. If you're speaking to your grandparents?
5. If you're speaking to your friend?
6. If you're speaking to the owners of a bakery?
7. If you're speaking to your parents?
8. If you're speaking to your dog?
9. If you're speaking to your sisters?
10. If you're speaking to the receptionist at an office?

**POINT 4:** INTRODUCING YOURSELF & OTHERS

*Salut!* In Part 1, you learned that this handy word means "Hello" or "Goodbye." It's a great way to greet your friends, and it's a great way to bring us to the next point, which is introductions. So, please go to your mirror, fix up your hair a bit, and say:

—*Bonjour, je m'appelle Madame Jeanne Durant. Comment vous appelez-vous ?*

—Hello, my name is Mrs. Jeanne Durant. What is you name?

And since it's only polite to respond when a stranger introduces herself to you, you should answer:

—*Enchanté(e) Madame. Je m'appelle_____.*

—Pleased to meet you, Ma'am. My name is_____.

Notice that there's an optional *-e* after *enchanté*. If you're a woman, you'd put it there. If you're a man, you wouldn't. We'll come back to that later, and it doesn't change pronunciation anyway.

Of course, if the person in the mirror is a man, he might say to you:
—*Bonjour, je m'appelle Monsieur Richard Dupont. Comment vous appelez-vous ?*
—Hello, my name is Mr. Richard Dupont. What is your name?

And you should answer him:
—*Enchanté(e) Monsieur. Je m'appelle_____.*
—Pleased to meet you, Sir. My name is_____.

This exciting dialogue involves characters who don't know each other and remain rather formal. That's typical between adults at work, in a store, at school, etc. The fact that the woman introduces herself as *Madame* So-and-So and the man as *Monsieur* So-and-So is an obvious hint that you have to remain formal. Now, let's try to cool down the atmosphere a bit . . . Go back to the mirror, and say:
—*Salut, je m'appelle Jeanne Durant. Et toi, comment t'appelles-tu ?*
—Hi, My name is Jeanne Durant. And you, what's your name?

Your answer is:
—*Enchanté(e) . Moi, je m'appelle_____.*
—Pleasure! My name is_____.

Or, you may be more of a Rich than a Jane:
—*Salut, je m'appelle Richard Dupont. Et toi, comment t'appelles-tu ?*
—Hi, My name is Richard Dupont. And you, what's your name?
—*Enchanté(e) . Moi, je m'appelle_____.*
—Pleasure! My name is_____.

Great. That's easy enough. That's the version you'll be using when you meet someone through a friend, or somehow through your circle. After introducing yourself, you may also want to introduce the person standing next to you. (Or not, but let's pretend you do, since it's polite.)

—*Et je vous présente Monsieur Pierre Dufour.*

—*Enchanté(e) Monsieur.*

—And this is Mr. Pierre Dufour. (literally, "And I introduce Mr. Peter Dufour to you.")

—Pleasure to meet you, Sir.

Of course, that's very formal, as you can tell by the *vous*. If you're introducing someone to a friend, you could say:

—*Et je te présente Pierre Dufour.*

—*Enchanté(e) Pierre.*

—And this is Pierre Dufour.

—Pleasure, Peter.

By the way, the expression *enchanté* (for a male speaker ) or *enchantée* (for a female speaker) is very common in French. It literally means "enchanted" or "charmed", but it's the equivalent of "pleased to meet you". The whole expression is:

—*Enchanté de faire votre connaissance.*

—Pleased to make your acquaintance.

The shorter version is just as good, though!

**POINT 5:** HOW ARE YOU ? . . .

We've covered a lot in this section already: *bonjour, bonsoir, je m'appelle, enchanté(e), je te/vous présente* . . . and much more. That's all very *formidable*! Now, let's look at the ways of expressing how you are, if you are well, or not so well, and how to ask how others are doing.

You'll notice that where English uses the verb "to be" in "how are you?" French uses the verb *aller*, which means "to go." And the *tu/vous* situation applies here, *naturellement*!

—*Comment allez-vous ?*

—How are you? (formal)

—*Comment vas-tu ?*

—How are you? (informal)

The answer to that question, regardless of *tu* or *vous* could be:

—*Je vais bien, merci.*

—I am well, thank you.

or . . .

—*Je vais très bien, merci.*

—I am very well, thank you.

or . . .

—*Je ne vais pas bien.*

—I am not well.

or . . .

—*Je vais mal.*

—I am not well.

There is an other rather casual way to say this, the equivalent of "how are you doing?" or "how's it going?"

—*Comment ça va ?*
—How are you doing?

The answer to this could be, from the best state to the worst:
—*Ça va très bien.*
—*Ça va bien.*
—*Ça va.*
—*Ça ne va pas mal.*
—*Ça va mal.*

They mean: I am doing very well, well, OK, not bad, not good . . . Of course, you could also say:
—*Comme ci, comme ça . . .*
—So so . . .

or . . .
—*Formidable!*
—Great! / Fantastic!

or . . .
—*Super !*
—Super!

You could also return the courtesy and add, "and you?"
—*Ça va très bien, merci . Et toi ?*
—I am very well, thank you. And you? (informal)
—*Je vais très bien, merci. Et vous ?*
—I'm very well, thanks. And you?

Another way to ask how someone is, in a friendly and familiar way, is to say:

—*Quoi de neuf ?*

—What's new?

### PRACTICE EXERCISE 3

Write the words in the right order to get sentences that make sense.

1. *allez / -vous / Comment / ?*
2. *Merci, / très / vais / je / bien.*
3. *toi, / Et / ça / comment / va / ?*
4. *Ça / ne / mal / va / pas.*
5. *Bonjour / Marie / -tu / comment / vas / ?*
6. *Je / mal / vais.*
7. *toujours / mal / vas / Tu.*
8. *je / Moi, / toujours / vais / bien.*

( **WATCH THE DVD** )

And now, time to review Part 2, Section A on your DVD! Of course, if you haven't digested all of this, just go back and read again. It's up to you. When you're through, you'll have some nice review exercises waiting for you!

# *REVIEW EXERCISES*

### REVIEW EXERCISE 1

Connect a phrase on the left with a phrase on the right to make a complete greeting.

1. *Luc, salut !...*            *... Et toi ?*
2. *Ça ne va pas mal ...*       *... enchantés, Mademoiselle.*
3. *Je vais bien, merci.*       *... Enchanté de faire votre connaissance.*
   *Voici ...*

4. *Bonjour Monsieur,*      *. . . Comment ça va ?*
   *Madame . . .*
5. *Je vous présente . . .*      *. . . mes parents.*
6. *Nous sommes . . .*      *. . . mon amie Nathalie.*

### REVIEW EXERCISE 2

Translate the following into English.

1. *Bonsoir. Je m'appelle Antoine.*
2. *Je te présente Frédéric.*
3. *Enchanté !*
4. *Comment ça va ?*
5. *Je vais très bien, merci. Et vous ?*
6. *Je m'appelle Richard, et je vous présente Marianne et Luc.*
7. *Salut, Étienne !*

# *Answer Key*

### PRACTICE EXERCISE 1

**1.** enchanté(e) – pleased to meet you  **2.** aller – to go  **3.** comment – how  **4.** le pays – the country  **5.** l'ami – the friend  **6.** nous – we  **7.** formidable – great  **8.** les États-Unis – The United States  **9.** salut – hello  **10.** présenter – to introduce

### PRACTICE EXERCISE 2

**1.** vous  **2.** tu  **3.** vous  **4.** vous (it's familiar, but plurall)  **5.** tu  **6.** vous  **7.** vous (again, plural familiar.)  **8.** tu  **9.** vous  **10.** vous

### PRACTICE EXERCISE 3

**1.** Comment allez-vous ?  **2.** Merci, je vais très bien.  **3.** Et toi, comment ça va ?  **4.** Ça ne va pas mal.  **5.** Bonjour Marie, comment vas –tu ?  **6.** Je vais mal.  **7.** Tu vas toujours mal.  **8.** Moi, je vais toujours bien.

## REVIEW EXERCISE 1

**1.** Luc, salut ! … Comment ça va ? … **2.** Ça ne va pas mal. … Et toi ? **3.** Je vais bien, merci. Voici … mes parents. **4.** Bonjour Monsieur, Madame … Enchanté de faire votre connaissance **5.** Je vous présente … mon amie Nathalie. **6.** Nous sommes … enchantés, Mademoiselle.

## REVIEW EXERCISE 2

**1.** Good Evening / Hello. My name is Antoine. **2.** This is Frederic. / I'd like to introduce Frederic to you. / Let me introduce Frederic to you. **3.** Pleased to meet you! / Pleasure meeting you! **4.** How are you? / How are you doing? / How's it going? **5.** I'm very well, thanks. And you? / I'm fine, thanks. And you? **6.** My name is Richard, and this is Marianne and Luc. / I'm Richard, and I'd like to introduce Marianne and Luc. **7.** Hi, Étienne! / Hello, Étienne!

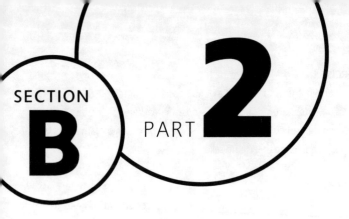

## Introduction to –er Verbs

Part 2 is called *Mes Préférences*, and the best way to talk about your preferences is with verbs like "love," "hate," "prefer," and "adore." In French, that's *aimer*, *détester*, *préférer*, and *adorer*. Isn't that easy? Let's start with some more vocabulary.

**POINT 1:** VOCABULARY

| | |
|---|---|
| *jamais* | never |
| *rien* | nothing |
| *tout* | everything |
| *tout le monde* | everybody |
| *préférer* | to prefer |
| *aimer* | to like / to love |
| *adorer* | to adore |
| *détester* | to hate |
| *danser* | to dance |
| *regarder* | to watch |
| *écouter* | to listen to |
| *la musique* | music |
| *classique* | classical |

| | |
|---|---|
| *le rap* | rap / rap music |
| *le rock* | rock / rock music |
| *le jazz* | jazz |
| *la techno* | techno |
| *la radio* | the radio |
| *la stéréo* | the stereo |
| *la télé(vision)* | the TV |
| *le théâtre* | the theater |
| *le ciné(ma)* | the movies |
| *la lumière* | the light |
| *le son* | the sound |
| *le restaurant* | the restaurant |
| *l'université* | the university / the college |
| *l'école* | school |
| *le collège* | junior high school |
| *le lycée* | high school |
| *le professeur* | the professor / teacher |
| *un étudiant* | a student (masculine) |
| *une étudiante* | a student (feminine) |
| *le sport* | sports |
| *le foot(ball)* | soccer |
| *le ballon* | the ball |
| *le jour* | the day |
| *la nuit* | the night |
| *le matin* | the morning |
| *le soir* | the evening |
| *tous les jours* | everyday |

## PRACTICE EXERCISE 1

1. Four words related to sports or physical activity are: _____,
   _____, _____, _____.

2. Three types of music are: _____, _____, _____.

3.  Three different levels of school are: _____, _____,
    _____.
4.  "Day and Night" is: _____ *et* _____.
5.  One place where a person can eat is: _____.
6.  If someone asks *Comment vas-tu ?* you might answer: *Je* _____, *bien,*
    *merci.*
7.  Two words related to culture are _____ and _____.
8.  Three examples of verbs are: _____, _____, _____.
9.  In a university class, you have *les* _____ who are studying and *le*
    _____ who is teaching.
10. *Adorer* is the opposite of _____.
11. The sun, or *le soleil*, gives us *la* _____.
12. *Au football*, players run after *un* _____.
13. *Le* _____ is after the afternoon, or the *après-midi*, but before *la nuit.*
14. Many people *aiment regarder la* _____ *tous les jours.*

---

**POINT 2:** INTRODUCTION TO -*ER* VERBS

Do you remember those verbs in the vocabulary list? Here they are again:
*aimer, adorer, préférer, détester.* Do you notice anything special about
them? Here's a hint – look at the endings. That's right, they all end in –*er*,
which makes them, well, –*er* verbs. Don't worry that the name of this verb
category is not very imaginative. More important is that they're nice,
predictable, regular verbs, which means that they follow a nice, predictable,
regular conjugation pattern.

Whoa! "Conjugation pattern?" Again, take your finger off the panic button.
You already know what this is. In English, take a verb like "to speak." Now,
use the right form of "to speak" after: I _____, you _____, he
_____, she _____, we _____, and they _____.
Without thinking about it, you said: "I speak," "you speak," "we speak," and

"they speak," but "he speaks" and "she speaks." That's a conjugation pattern. You change the forms of a verb depending on who or what's doing the action of the verb.

French is the same way. But the conjugation is a bit more complicated, and there are actually a few different patterns, depending on which category the verb belongs to. But don't worry. We're sticking to regular –er verbs, and in fact, we're only sticking to the I (*je*) and you (*tu*) forms for now.

## PRACTICE EXERCISE 2

You've already seen quite a few verbs in this course, believe it or not. Do you remember them? Can you figure out the meaning of a few verbs you haven't seen yet? Connect the French verbs on the left with their meanings on the right.

1. *danser*          to go
2. *adorer*          to speak
3. *préférer*        to dance
4. *détester*        to listen to
5. *aimer*           to adore
6. *regarder*        to hate
7. *aller*           to prefer
8. *écouter*         to watch
9. *parler*          to sing
10. *chanter*        to like / to love

## POINT 3: THE INFINITIVE & THE *JE* AND *TU* PERSONS

The infinitive is easy. It's the form of the verb that's not conjugated. In English, the infinitive of the verb is preceded by "to" (to like, to live, to love, to prevaricate, to filibuster, etc.) In French, the infinitive can have a few possible endings, but we're only going to look at –er verbs, such as *aimer*.

To conjugate an –er verb, drop the –er ending, and to the remaining stem (aim-) add –e for the je form, and –es for the tu form. Simple, right? And better yet, they're both even pronounced exactly the same way.

*aimer* (to like/love)  *j'aime* (I like/love)  *tu aimes* (you like/love)

—*J'aime la musique classique.*
—I like classical music.
—*Tu aimes le théâtre.*
—You like theater.

Did you notice that *je* became *j'* before *aime*? That's just because French always likes to sound as pretty as possible, and pronouncing the two vowels together (*je* + *aime*) would be clunky and not very pretty at all. *J'aime* runs together so smoothly, so nicely . . . But let's look at some other examples.

*adorer* (to adore)  *j'adore* (I adore)  *tu adores* (you adore)

—*J'adore le jazz.*
—I love jazz.
—*Tu adores le cinéma.*
—You love movies.

*préférer* (to prefer)  *je préfère* (I prefer)  *tu préfères* (you prefer)

—*Je préfère la musique rap.*
—I prefer rap music.
—*Tu préfères la danse.*
—You prefer dance.

Notice here that *je* stays *je*, because *préfère* starts with a consonant. And also note that the second é becomes è when you conjugate *préférer*. Don't worry about why for now – just remember it.

*détester* (to hate)     *je déteste* (I hate)     *tu détestes* (you hate)

—*Je déteste la techno.*
—I hate techno.
—*Tu détestes la télévision.*
—You hate TV.
—*Je parle français, et tu parles italien.*
—I speak French, and you speak Italian.
—*Je chante bien, et tu chantes mal.*
—I sing well, and you sing poorly.

## POINT 4: THE ELISION

Let's talk for a second again about *je* vs. *j'*. That's called "elision," or *élision*, and it happens quite a bit in French, not just with *je*. As you just saw, *je* loses its *e* in front of verbs like *aimer*, *adorer*, *écouter*, etc., in order to make the pronunciation smoother. And elision happens with other "small" words such as *me* (me), *te* (you), *se* (himself, herself, itself), *le* (the, it), *la* (the, it), *de* (of) and *ne* (not): *J'adore* (I adore), *l'université* (the university), *l'hôtel* (the hotel), *l'amie* (the girlfriend), *je m'appelle* (I'm called), *tu t'appelles* (you're called), *il n'aime pas* (he doesn't like.) Even the word *élision* is an example. *La élision* becomes *l'élision*!

## POINT 5: HOW TO SAY NO!

Before going any further, there is one thing you need to know, and I am sure you all will approve . . . *Non* ! Exactly! You must know how to say no! You've just learned how to express that you're doing something, so now let's take a look at how to express that you're not doing something.

In English, there is of course the word "no," which you already know is *non* in French. But if you want to make a verb negative, you use "not" in English. In French, you have to make a kind of negative verb sandwich, using *ne* and then the verb and then *pas*. Take a look at these examples:

—*Oui, j'aime la télévision.*
—Yes, I like television.
—*Non, je n'aime pas la télévision.*
—No, I don't like television.
—*Je déteste le sport.*
—I hate sports.
—*Je ne déteste pas le sport.*
—I don't hate sports.

See how the French negation *ne . . . pas* embraces the verb? Ah, these French . . . always hugging and embracing. And, did you notice that in the first example what is suppposed to be *ne . . . pas* wound up *n' . . . pas*? Can you guess why? You got it, it's that *élision* trick again! The word *ne* becomes *n'* because the verb starts with the vowel *a*.

French also has other ways to express negation, just like English. For example, what if you don't just "not" sing, but you "never" sing? Or, perhaps due to pressure from people who have heard you sing, you'll be doing that "not any more?"

*ne . . . plus*: no more / not any more
—*Tu ne détestes plus l'école ?*
—You don't hate school anymore?

*ne . . . jamais*: never / not ever
—*Je ne danse jamais.*
—I never dance. / I don't ever dance.

*ne . . . personne:* not anyone / nobody

—*Je n'aime personne.*

—I don't like anyone. / I like nobody.

*ne . . . rien:* nothing / not anything:

—*Tu n'écoutes rien.*

—You don't listen to anything. / You listen to nothing.

**PRACTICE EXERCISE 3**

Re-write each sentence in the negative.

1. *Tu aimes l'école.*
2. *Je préfère la danse.*
3. *J'adore ton ami.*
4. *Tu écoutes la radio.*
5. *Mon amie regarde la télévision.*
6. *Tu aimes la nature.*
7. *Je préfère la musique.*
8. *Moi, j'adore le sport.*
9. *J'écoute tout le monde.*
10. *Tu détestes tout.*

( **WATCH THE DVD** )

So that wasn't too hard, was it? Then watch Section B, Part 2 on your DVD, and of course come back to the book for a review.

# REVIEW EXERCISES

### REVIEW EXERCISE 1

Please translate the following sentences from French into English.

1. *J'aime le cinéma.*
2. *J'écoute la musique.*
3. *Je n'écoute pas la radio.*
4. *Je déteste la télévision.*
5. *Je préfère le sport.*
6. *Je ne regarde pas la télé.*
7. *Je n'aime pas la techno.*
8. *Je n'écoute personne.*

### REVIEW EXERCISE 2

Write these sentences in the negative.

1. *J'aime tout!*
2. *J'écoute la radio le matin.*
3. *Tu préfères le football.*
4. *Je vais à l'université.*
5. *Tu vas bien.*
6. *Tu aimes tout le monde.*
7. *Je regarde mon ami.*
8. *Je regarde la télévision tous les jours.*

# Answer Key

### PRACTICE EXERCISE 1

**1.** danser, le football, le ballon, le sport  **2.** la musique classique, le rock, la techno, la musique jazz (le jazz) . . . **3.** l'école, le collège, le lycée, l'université **4.** (le) jour et (la) nuit **5.** le restaurant **6.** vais **7.** le théâtre, la danse, le cinéma, la musique  **8.** aimer, danser, regarder, écouter, adorer, détester, préférer, chanter  **9.** étudiants, professeur  **10.** détester  **11.** lumière  **12.** ballon  **13.** soir  **14.** télévision

## PRACTICE EXERCISE 2

**1.** danser – to dance  **2.** adorer – to adore  **3.** préférer – to prefer  **4.** détester – to hate  **5.** aimer – to like / to love  **6.** regarder – to watch  **7.** aller – to go  **8.** écouter – to listen to  **9.** parler – to speak  **10.** chanter – to sing

## PRACTICE EXERCISE 3

**1.** Tu n'aimes pas l'école.  **2.** Je ne préfère pas la danse.  **3.** Je n'adore pas ton ami.  **4.** Tu n'écoutes pas la radio.  **5.** Mon amie ne regarde pas la télévision.  **6.** Tu n'aimes pas la nature.  **7.** Je ne préfère pas la musique.  **8.** Moi, je n'adore pas le sport.  **9.** Je n'écoute pas tout le monde.  **10.** Tu ne détestes pas tout.

## REVIEW EXERCISE 1

**1.** I like/love the movies.  **2.** I listen to music. / I'm listening to music.  **3.** I don't listen to the radio. / I'm not listening to the radio.  **4.** I hate television.  **5.** I prefer sports.  **6.** I don't watch television. / I'm not watching television.  **7.** I don't like techno.  **8.** I don't listen to anyone. / I'm not listening to anyone. / I listen to nobody.

## REVIEW EXERCISE 2

**1.** Je n'aime rien ! / Je n'aime pas tout !  **2.** Je n'écoute pas la radio le matin.  **3.** Tu ne préfères pas le football.  **4.** Je ne vais pas à l'université.  **5.** Tu ne vas pas bien.  **6.** Tu n'aimes personne. / Tu n'aimes pas tout le monde.  **7.** Je ne regarde pas mon ami.  **8.** Je ne regarde pas la télévision tous les jours.

## *Getting Infinitives into Action*

In the last section you learned a lot of infinitives – the "to" form of a verb that you've seen as an *–er* form in French. In this section you're going to learn how to work with those forms, or rather, how to make them work for you! But first, some vocabulary.

**POINT 1:** VOCABULARY

| | |
|---|---|
| *écouter* | to listen to |
| *regarder* | to look at / to watch |
| *étudier* | to study |
| *jouer* | to play |
| *danser* | to dance |
| *la danse* | dance |
| *le spectacle de danse* | dance performance |
| *le concert* | the concert |
| *le match de football* | the soccer game |
| *marcher* | to walk / to work (as in "to function") |
| *ça marche!* | that works! / okay! |
| *changer* | to change |
| *chanter* | to sing |

| *la chanson* | the song |
| *toujours* | always |
| *jamais* | never |
| *avec* | with |
| *à la radio* | on the radio |
| *à la télé* | on TV |

**PRACTICE EXERCISE 1**

Fill in the blanks.

1. *J'aime les _____ de danse.*
2. *Tu adores regarder les _____ de football à la télévision.*
3. *Je n'écoute pas tout le monde ; je n'écoute _____.*
4. *Je n'aime pas tout ; je n'aime _____.*
5. *Je chante une _____.*
6. *À l'université, tu _____ le français.*
7. *Oui, c'est bien ! Ça _____ !*
8. *Mon ami aime les _____ de musique classique.*

## POINT 2: USING THOSE INFINITIVES

In English, you can use "to dance" after verbs like "like" or "love" or "hate." In French, you can do the same thing, using all sorts of infinitives after *aimer, adorer, préférer,* and *détester.* Take a look:

—*J'adore étudier.*
—I love to study.
—*Tu aimes regarder les matchs de football à la télévision.*
—You like to watch the soccer games on TV.

Notice that in these examples, the infinitive doesn't change forms. In other words, you only conjugate the main verb, and then leave that infinitive alone!

—*Je n'aime pas marcher.*
—I don't like to walk.
—*Tu adores aller au cinéma avec des amis.*
—You love to go to the movies with (some) friends.
—*Je préfère danser.*
—I prefer to dance.
—*Mon ami déteste regarder la télévision.*
—My friend hates watching TV.
—*Et moi, j'adore écouter la musique classique à la radio.*
—And I love to listen to classical music on the radio.

**PRACTICE EXERCISE 2**

Combine the following pairs of sentences. For example:

*Je regarde le match de football. J'aime ça.* (I like that.)
*J'aime regarder le match de football.*

1. *Tu chantes tous les jours. Tu aimes ça.*
2. *J'étudie. Je déteste ça.*
3. *Tu écoutes la radio le matin. Tu adores ça.*
4. *Je chante l'opéra. Je préfère ça.*
5. *Je marche. Je n'aime pas ça.*
6. *Tu danses. Tu ne détestes pas ça.*

Yes, it's time to go to your DVD and watch Section C of Part 2.

# *REVIEW EXERCISES*

### REVIEW EXERCISE 1

Translate the following sentences from French into English.

1. *J'adore aller au cinéma.*
2. *Je n'aime pas regarder la télé.*
3. *Tu détestes aller à l'université.*
4. *Mais tu aimes étudier.*
5. *Ou tu préfères jouer au football.*
6. *Je préfère marcher et danser.*
7. *Je ne déteste rien.*
8. *J'adore écouter la musique à la radio.*

### REVIEW EXERCISE 2

Connect the two parts of each split sentence.

1. *J'adore aller à la . . .*      *rien.*
2. *Tu aimes marcher . . .*      *match de foot.*
3. *Tu n'aimes pas*      *dans New York*
   *regarder le sport . . .*
4. *Tu préfères aller au . . .*      *danse.*
5. *Je ne déteste . . .*      *le français.*
6. *J'aime étudier . . .*      *à la télévision.*

## REVIEW EXERCISE 3

Translate these sentences from English into French.

1. You like to dance.
2. You go to the university every day.
3. I adore classical music concerts. (concerts of classical music.)
4. You don't listen to rock songs any more.
5. I prefer walking in New York (*dans New York.*)
6. I hate watching television. (I hate to watch television.)

# *Answer Key*

### PRACTICE EXERCISE 1

**1.** spectacles **2.** matchs **3.** personne **4.** rien **5.** chanson **6.** étudies **7.** marche **8.** concerts

### PRACTICE EXERCISE 2

**1.** Tu aimes chanter tous les jours. **2.** Je déteste étudier. **3.** Tu adores écouter la radio le matin. **4.** Je préfère chanter l'opéra. **5.** Je n'aime pas marcher. **6.** Tu ne détestes pas danser.

### REVIEW EXERCISE 1

**1.** I love to go to the movies. **2.** I don't like to watch TV. **3.** You hate to go to the university. **4.** But you like to study. **5.** Or you prefer to play soccer. **6.** I prefer to walk and dance. **7.** I don't hate anything. **8.** I love to listen to music on the radio.

### REVIEW EXERCISE 2

**1.** J'adore aller à la . . . danse. **2.** Tu aimes marcher . . . dans New York **3.** Tu n'aimes pas regarder le sport . . . à la télévision **4.** Tu préfères aller au … match de foot. **5.** Je ne déteste … rien. **6.** J'aime étudier … le français.

### REVIEW EXERCISE 3

**1.** Tu aimes danser. **2.** Tu vas à l'université tous les jours. **3.** J'adore les concerts de musique classique. **4.** Tu n'écoutes plus les chansons de rock. **5.** Je préfère marcher dans New York. **6.** Je déteste regarder la télévision.

## *Gender and Definite Articles*

You've noticed all along that there's more than one way to say "the" in French. In this section we're going to take a closer look at that, and introduce you to the concept of gender, or why a bridge is masculine but a street is feminine! No, there's nothing Freudian about it. Just grammar. But first, let's learn some new words.

**POINT 1:** VOCABULARY

| | |
|---|---|
| *le, la, les, l'* | the |
| *alors* | so |
| *dans* | in |
| *mais* | but |
| *très* | very |
| *voici* | here is , this is |
| *la reine* | the queen |
| *le roi* | the king |
| *le président* | the president |
| *le maire* | the mayor |
| *la ville* | the city / the town |
| *la rue* | the street |

| | |
|---|---|
| *le pont* | the bridge |
| *l'Angleterre* | England |
| *la nature* | nature |
| *la bicyclette* | the bicycle |
| *le bureau* | the office / the desk |
| *le matin* | the morning |
| *la journée / le jour* | the day |
| *la nuit* | the night |
| *le soir* | the evening |
| *la boulangerie* | the bakery |
| *le marché* | the market |
| *le supermarché* | the supermarket |
| *le marché aux puces* | the flea market |
| *la chance* | chance |
| *beau* | beautiful (masc.) |
| *belle* | beautiful (fem.) |

## PRACTICE EXERCISE 1

Connect the French words on the left with their English equivalents on the right.

| | | |
|---|---|---|
| 1. | *alors* | the supermarket |
| 2. | *mais* | the office / the desk |
| 3. | *voici* | the flea market |
| 4. | *le maire* | the day |
| 5. | *la ville* | nature |
| 6. | *la rue* | the bakery |
| 7. | *le pont* | the evening |
| 8. | *la nature* | here is , this is |
| 9. | *la bicyclette* | but |
| 10. | *le bureau* | the mayor |
| 11. | *le matin* | so |
| 12. | *la journée* | the morning |

| 13. | *le soir* | the street |
|-----|-----------|------------|
| 14. | *la boulangerie* | the bridge |
| 15. | *le supermarché* | the bicycle |
| 16. | *le marché aux puces* | the city / the town |

### PRACTICE EXERCISE 2

Fill in the blanks in the following sentences:

1. *Le* _____ runs *la ville*.
2. I can buy some *croissants* and some bread *à la* _____
3. *La* _____ is the same as *le jour*.
4. *J'aime marcher dans les* _____ *de la ville*.
5. *La* _____ *et* the bicycle are the same thing.
6. At the _____ you can buy all kinds of food and other things.
7. _____ *mon ami Carlos*.
8. 7:00 am is *le matin* and 7:00 pm is *le* _____

## POINT 2: WHAT IS A GENDER?

Now, are you ready for the concept of gender? All nouns in French – man, woman, table, chair, life, liberty – have gender. The gender of a noun may sound like its "sex," and that wouldn't be too far off base in the case of animate nouns like "man" or "woman." But when you're talking about tables and chairs, the comparison breaks down a bit. So, think of gender as "grammatical category." All nouns in French fall into one of two grammatical categories; a noun in French can be either feminine (fem.) or masculine (masc.). And depending on that gender, the article (the little word preceding the noun in a sentence, such as "the" or "a") will be feminine or masculine.

Here's a tip. Remember to learn each new noun with its article right from the start. There's no rule that works 100% of the time to determine whether a noun is feminine or masculine. You just have to memorize it, so remember that *le* or *la*, *un* or *une* right at the get-go.

There are, however, some cases where you can be almost sure of the gender of a noun. First of all, animate, or living, nouns take their natural gender. For example, *homme* (man), *garçon* (boy), *père* (father), and *taureau* (bull) are all masculine. And *femme* (woman), *fille* (girl), *mère* (mother) and *vache* (cow) are all feminine. So, you can also guess the genders of *sœur* (sister), *frère* (brother), *poule* (hen), and *coq* (rooster).

Your second clue will come from the ending of the noun. Nouns ending in -*ette*, -*ère*, -*ée*, -*rie*, -*ance*, -*ence* and -*ion* are usually feminine. (And note that it's only usually! It's not foolproof!) So, these nouns are all feminine: *bicyclette* (bicycle), *dance* (dance), *journée* (day), *boulangerie* (bakery), *préférence* (preference), *lumière* (light), *télévision* (television), and *introduction* (introduction).

Nouns ending in -*ant*, -*ent*, -*on*, -*ont* are usually masculine. So, these nouns are masculine: *restaurant* (restaurant), *président* (president), *son* (sound), *pont* (bridge).

But again, these "rules" aren't 100% reliable, so the best technique is still to learn each noun with its gender. And the easiest way to do that is to memorize each new noun with its article. Which brings us to . . .

### POINT 3: THE DEFINITE ARTICLES

There are two types of articles, definite and indefinite. Definite articles point to something specific, or definite, and indefinite articles point to something indefinite (or "any old . . .") You may have guessed, or you may already know, that the definite article in English is "the," and the indefinite article is "a" (or "an" before a vowel sound.) Right now, let's concentrate on the definite articles in French.

The French definite article varies according to the gender of the noun in the singular form. The forms are *le* for singular masculine nouns, and *la* for singular feminine nouns. Both *le* and *la* become *l'* when there is an elision before a vowel or silent *h*.

| | |
|---|---|
| *le sport* | the sports |
| *l'ami* | the (masculine) friend |
| *le théâtre* | the theater |
| *le cinéma* | the movies |
| *l'hôtel* | the hotel |
| *la musique* | the music |
| *la radio* | the radio |
| *l'université* | the university |

But it gets easier in the plural. Everything becomes *les*.

| | |
|---|---|
| *les amis* | the friends |
| *les théâtres* | the theaters |
| *les radios* | the radios |
| *les hôtels* | the hotels |
| *les universités* | the universities |
| *les cinémas* | the movies |

Did you notice how simple it is to form the plural in French? It's pretty much just like English; you add an –*s* to the end of a word. *Le théâtre* becomes *les théâtres*, and *l'ami* becomes *les amis*. And as a bonus, you don't even pronounce the plural any differentlyl But you can always tell if it's plural, because you'll hear *les* instead of *le, la,* or *l'*.

Of course, any self respecting language has a few surprises up its sleeve, so naturally, there are some cases where the plural is formed in different ways.

But don't be indignant. English is the same. Think: city/cities, fish/fish, child/children, ox/oxen, tooth/teeth! We won't even get into the other kinds of plurals in French for now. (But they're not as whacky as English.) Instead, let's practice the definite articles.

## PRACTICE EXERCISE 3

Write *le, la, l'*, or *les* before each of the following nouns.

1. _____ *université*
2. _____ *mère*
3. _____ *ballons*
4. _____ *sport*
5. _____ *radios*
6. _____ *nature*
7. _____ *jour*
8. _____ *télé*
9. _____ *pères*
10. _____ *ciné*
11. _____ *musique*
12. _____ *ami*
13. _____ *villes*
14. _____ *maire*
15. _____ *sœur*
16. _____ *sœurs*
17. _____ *universités*

## PRACTICE EXERCISE 4

Now complete each sentence with the correct article.

1. _____ *professeur aime* _____ *musique classique.*
2. *Je préfère regarder* _____ *télévision.*
3. *Je déteste* _____ *football.*
4. *Mon ami écoute* _____ *stéréo. Il aime* _____ *jazz.*
5. _____ *étudiant ne joue plus.*

6. _____ professeur aime aller au cinéma avec _____ étudiants.

7. Tu écoutes _____ musique rap à _____ radio.

8. Je danse et je chante avec _____ amis.

## POINT 4: WHAT'S WITH ALL OF THOSE ARTICLES?

One last note before we go back to your favorite DVD. Did you notice in the exercise above that the French have a love affair with the definite article? "The professor likes the classical music." "I prefer watching the television." "I hate the soccer." "My friend is listening to the radio. He likes the jazz." It sounds weird in English, right? Well, then it's a good thing it's not English!

In French, it would sound weird not to use the definite articles that much. French doesn't like "naked nouns," so nouns in French are usually dressed up with an article, even when the poor noun would be left naked and out in the cold in English. We won't bore you with all of the rules, but just notice the difference.

## WATCH THE DVD

And now, back to that DVD, Part 2 Section D! And come back for more review exercises!

# REVIEW EXERCISES

### REVIEW EXERCISE 1
Translate the following words and phrases.

1. *la musique à la radio*

2. *le pont et la rue*

3. *le sport*
4. *les étudiants et les professeurs à l'université*
5. *la reine et le roi*
6. *le marché aux puces*
7. *la mère et le père*
8. *le jour et la nuit*

## REVIEW EXERCISE 2

Connect a phrase in the left hand column to a phrase in the right hand column to form a logical sentence.

1. *Le maire aime*      *la télévision.*
2. *Mon ami regarde*      *Sonja George.*
3. *Je préfère*      *jamais.*
4. *Et toi, comment*      *comme ci , comme ça.*
5. *J'adore chanter*      *étudier à l'université.*
6. *Je m'appelle*      *la ville.*
7. *Tu n'écoutes*      *vas-tu ?*
8. *Ça va*      *et danser.*

## REVIEW EXERCISE 3

*Vrai ou Faux?* True or False?

1. V   F     To say that the dog, *le chien*, is beautiful, you'd use *belle*.
2. V   F     *La ville* is run by *le maire*.
3. V   F     *Le supermarché et le marché aux puces* are the same things.
4. V   F     The two genders in French are singular and plural.
5. V   F     The feminine definite article is *la* or *l'*.
6. V   F     *Le bureau* is where you buy bread.
7. V   F     You use *l'* for both singular and plural.
8. V   F     Genders in French follow regular rules.

# Answer Key

## PRACTICE EXERCISE 1

**1.** alors – so **2.** mais – but **3.** voici- here is, this is **4.** le maire – the mayor **5.** la ville – the city / the town **6.** la rue – the street **7.** le pont – the bridge **8.** la nature – nature **9.** la bicyclette – the bicycle **10.** le bureau – the office / the desk **11.** le matin – the morning **12.** la journée – the day **13.** le soir – the evening **14.** la boulangerie – the bakery **15.** le supermarché – the supermarket **16.** la marché aux puces – the flea market

## PRACTICE EXERCISE 2

**1.** maire. **2.** boulangerie. **3.** journée. **4.** rues. **5.** bicyclette. **6.** supermarché. **7.** Voici. **8.** soir.

## PRACTICE EXERCISE 3

**1.** l'université **2.** la mère **3.** les ballons **4.** le sport **5.** les radios **6.** la nature **7.** le jour **8.** la télé **9.** les pères **10.** le ciné **11.** la musique **12.** l'ami **13.** les villes **14.** le maire **15.** la sœur **16.** les sœurs **17.** les universités

## PRACTICE EXERCISE 4

**1.** Le/la. **2.** la.. **3.** le. **4.** la/le. **5.** L'. **6.** Le/les **7.** la/la. **8.** les.

## REVIEW EXERCISE 1

**1.** the music on the radio **2.** the bridge and the street **3.** the sports (or: sports) **4.** the students and the professors at the university **5.** the queen and the king **6.** the flea market **7.** the mother and the father **8.** the day and the night

## REVIEW EXERCISE 2

**1.** Le maire aime la ville. **2.** Mon ami regarde la télévision. **3.** Je préfère étudier à l'université. **4.** Et toi, comment vas-tu ? **5.** J'adore chanter et danser.  **6.** Je m'appelle Sonja George.  **7.** Tu n'écoutes jamais.  **8.** Ça va comme ci, comme ça.

## REVIEW EXERCISE 3

**1.** FAUX: You'd use beau, since le chien is masculine  **2.** VRAI  **3.** FAUX: Le supermarché is a supermarket, and marché aux puces is a flea market.  **4.** FAUX: The two genders in French are masculine and feminine.  **5.** VRAI  **6.** FAUX: Le bureau is the office. You buy bread at la boulangerie.  **7.** FAUX: L' is only used in the singular. It becomes les in the plural.  **8.** FAUX: Genders in French do not follow regular rules all the time.

# Ma Famille

PART **3**

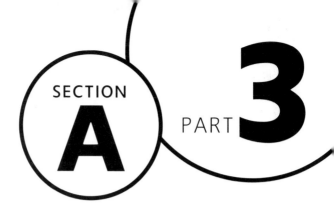

SECTION **A** PART **3**

# *Subject Pronouns*

The name of Part 3 is *Ma Famille* – another one you can guess at, right? "My Family" will give you everything you need to impress (or annoy) your relatives, because soon you'll be able to talk about everyone in your family! You'll also learn about pronouns and the verb *être* (to be), and you'll see how to put adjectives to work for you. Sound like it's getting serious? Not really, since we'll take it all one step at a time. As usual, we'll start with some new words.

**POINT 1:** VOCABULARY

Here are some words to ease you into Part 3.    Some of them are already familiar by now, so you can take them as free-bee's. And you'll notice that with the adjectives, there are two possible endings. For example, for "big" you'll see *grand, -e.* That means that there are two forms: *grand* and *grande.* You can probably guess by now that one is masculine and the other is feminine, right? We'll get a little deeper into that very soon!

| | |
|---|---|
| *un peu (de . . . )* | a little (of . . . ) |
| *beaucoup (de . . . )* | a lot (of . . . ) |
| *aussi* | also |
| *moi* | me |

| | |
|---|---|
| *qui* | who |
| *voilà* | there is / there are , this is / these are |
| *ici* | here |
| *là* | there |
| *sur* | on |
| *sous* | under |
| *dans* | in |
| *de* | of |
| *parler* | to speak |
| *étudiant* | student (masc.) |
| *étudiante* | student (fem.) |
| *les parents* | the parents |
| *la mère* | the mother |
| *le père* | the father |
| *le frère* | the brother |
| *la sœur* | the sister |
| *la chambre* | the bedroom |
| *la fenêtre* | the window |
| *sympa(thique)* | cool, friendly |
| *mince* | thin |
| *petit, -e* | small, little |
| *joli, -e* | pretty |
| *vert, -e* | green |
| *grand, -e* | tall, big |
| *gros, -se* | fat, big |
| *gentil, -le* | nice, kind |
| *heureux, -euse* | happy |
| *malheureux, -euse* | unhappy |
| *paresseux, -euse* | lazy |
| *travailleur, -euse* | hard working |

## PRACTICE EXERCISE 1

1. If I am t*a sœur*, what are you? Here's a clue – there are two possibilities. If you're a girl, you're *ma* _____, but if you're a boy, you're *mon* _____

2. The opposite of *grand et gros* is: _____ *et* _____

3. What color is *la plante*? _____ (Use the form with the *–e* ending!)

4. In order to get good grades, *un étudiant* has to be: _____.

5. In France, there's a saying: "All that is little is pretty." *Tout ce qui est petit est* _____. (Don't use the *–e* ending here.)

6. The opposite of *heureux* is: _____.

## PRACTICE EXERCISE 2

Find the opposite of the following words.

1. *mince* _____
2. *ici* _____
3. *sur* _____
4. *grand* _____
5. *malheureux* _____
6. *travailleur* _____
7. *un peu de* _____
8. *les enfants* _____

## **POINT 2:** THE SUBJECT PRONOUNS

Pronouns are little words that replace nouns: I, me, you, he, him, she, her, it, we, us, you, they, them … in English. Subject pronouns are the pronouns that you can use as the subject of a sentence. ("He" instead of "him" or "I" instead of "me," unless you make a habit of saying things like "Me want to eat now.") It should be pretty easy for you to memorize the subject pronouns in French, since you already know about the delicate case of *tu* and *vous* (both meaning "you"). As you remember, you use *vous* in formal or anonymous situations with adults, and *tu* with your friends, your family, and people of your age and younger. So, you've already got two of the pronouns covered. But, just like in English, there are other subject pronouns. Let's take a look at them:

| | |
|---|---|
| *je* | I |

No complication here. Just know that *je* is not capitalized except at the beginning of a sentence.

—*Je file.*

—I'm out of here.

| | |
|---|---|
| *tu* | you (familiar) |

—*Tu vas bien ?*

—You're doing well?

| | |
|---|---|
| *vous* | you (formal) |

—*Préférez-vous du café ou du thé ?*

—Do you prefer coffee or tea?

| | |
|---|---|
| *il* | he (or it) |

As you know, all French nouns have a gender, even inanimate objects. So, just as *le père* and *le frère* would be *il*, so too would *le pont* and *le bureau*! Sound bizarre? Don't worry, you'll get used to it!

—*Jean adore le sport ? Oui, il adore le sport.*

—John adores sports? Yes, he adores sports.

—*L'oiseau est bleu ? Oui, il est bleu.*

—The bird is blue? Yes, it's blue.

| | |
|---|---|
| *elle* | she (or it) |

—*Christelle étudie l'anglais ? Oui, elle étudie l'anglais.*

—Christelle is studying English? Yes, she's studying English.

—*La chambre est grande ? Oui, elle est grande.*

—The bedroom is big? Yes, it's big.

*on*                           one / "you" / "they" / we

*On* has a few different uses. First of all, it means "one" in a general sense, as in: "One should keep one's voice down in a library." Of course, few people really speak that way in English, and the more common way to say that would be: "You should keep your voice down in a library." Another general pronoun in English is "they," as in: "What language do they speak in Thailand?" *On* can be used in all of those cases – "one," "you," "they" in a general sense. But *on* can also mean "we" in conversational French.

—*On parle français en France.*

—They speak /one speaks French in France.

—*On regarde la télé ce soir.*

—We're watching TV tonight.


*nous*                    we

This is the more standard way to say "we."

—*Nous sommes cousins.*

—We are cousins.


*vous*                    you, formal and familiar plural.

—*Vous êtes le professeur ?*

—You're the professor?

—*Vous êtes mes grands-parents.*

—You are my grandparents.


*ils*                           they

One important thing to know about *ils* is that it's used to refer not just to a group of guys or masculine things, but also to a mixed group of men and women, boys and girls, masculine and feminine things, etc. Boy, this is a man's world!

—*Ils (Carlos et Richard) sont chez Momo.*

—They (Carlos and Richard) are at Momo's.

—*Ils (les oiseaux) chantent.*

—They (the birds) are singing.

—*Ils (mon frère et mes sœurs) sont dans ma chambre.*

—They (my brother and my sisters) are in my room.

—*Ils (le livre et la radio) sont dans ma chambre.*

—They (the book and the radio) are in my room.


*elles*                     they

*Elles* is just used for groups of feminine people, animals, or things.

—*Elles (Aziza et Aïcha) regardent la télé.*

—They (Aziza et Aïcha) are watching TV.

—*Elles (les robes) sont courtes.*

—They (the dresses) are short.


**PRACTICE EXERCISE 3**

Now let's practice. Match the French pronouns with their equivalents in English.

| | | |
|---|---|---|
| 1. | *tu* | we |
| 2. | *nous* | they |
| 3. | *elles* | he |
| 4. | *vous* | one, we, they |
| 5. | *il* | you, familiar |
| 6. | *je* | you, polite |
| 7. | *elle* | she |
| 8. | *on* | I |


**PRACTICE EXERCISE 4**

Now replace each of the following words or phrases with a pronoun.

1. *Michelle*

2. *le professeur*

3. *l'étudiante*

4. *l'étudiante et le professeur*

5. *ma sœur et mon frère*

6. *le chien*
7. *la radio et la télévision*
8. *la rue et le pont*
9. *Véronique et Natalie*
10. *François*

( **WATCH THE DVD** )

Isn't it time to review Part 3, Section A on your DVD? *Mais oui !*

# *REVIEW EXERCISES*

### REVIEW EXERCISE 1

Replace the English pronouns with French pronouns in the following sentences. You can see the translations of the sentences if you need a little boost.

1. (we) *regardons le match de foot ici.* (We watch the football match here.)
2. (she) *mange au restaurant avec son amie.* (She eats at the restaurant with her friend.)
3. *Quelquefois,* (I) *écoute la radio.* (Sometimes, I listen to the radio.)
4. (he) *est paresseux.* (He's lazy.)
5. (we) *sommes travailleurs.* (We are hardworking.)
6. (you) *t'appelles Carlos.* (Your name is Carlos.)
7. (he) *parle un peu français.* (He speaks a little French.)
8. (you) *es très gentil.* (You're nice.)

### REVIEW EXERCISE 2

Give the plural forms of the following singular pronouns.

1. *tu*
2. *je*
3. *elle*
4. *il*
5. *vous*

### REVIEW EXERCISE 3

Translate each of the following sentences into English. You'll notice some verb endings you haven't seen before, but since you know the pronouns now, you can figure out what they mean.

1. *Mon nom est Frédérique.*
2. *Et voici ma sœur, Marianne.*
3. *Et toi, comment t'appelles-tu ?*
4. *Mes parents parlent français et anglais.*
5. *Vous aimez aller au cinéma.*
6. *Oui, nous aimons aller au cinéma et au théâtre.*
7. *Comment vas-tu ?*
8. *Je vais bien, merci.*

## Answer Key

**PRACTICE EXERCISE 1**

**1.** sœur, frère  **2.** petit, mince  **3.** verte  **4.** travailleur  **5.** joli  **6.** malheureux

**PRACTICE EXERCISE 2**

**1.** gros  **2.** là  **3.** sous  **4.** petit  **5.** heureux  **6.** paresseux  **7.** beaucoup de  **8.** les parents

**PRACTICE EXERCISE 3**

**1.** tu – you, familiar  **2.** nous – we  **3.** elles – they  **4.** vous – you, polite  **5.** il – he
**6.** je – I  **7.** elle – she  **8.** on – one, we, they

**PRACTICE EXERCISE 4**

**1.** elle  **2.** il  **3.** elle  **4.** ils  **5.** ils  **6.** il  **7.** elles  **8.** ils  **9.** elles  **10.** il

**REVIEW EXERCISE 1**

**1.** Nous.  **2.** Elle.  **3.** j'.  **4.** Il.  **5.** Nous.  **6.** Tu.  **7.** Il.  **8.** Tu.

**REVIEW EXERCISE 2**

**1.** vous  **2.** nous  **3.** elles  **4.** ils  **5.** vous

**REVIEW EXERCISE 3**

**1.** My name is Frédérique.  **2.** And this is (here is) my sister Marianne.  **3.** And you, what's your name?  **4.** My parents speak French and English.  **5.** You like to go to the movies.  **6.** Yes, we like to go to the movies and to the theatre.  **7.** How are you?  **8.** I am well (fine), thank you.

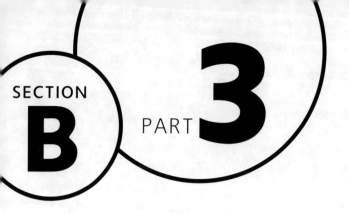

## *The Verb* ÊTRE

**POINT 1:** VOCABULARY

| | |
|---|---|
| *chez* | at (someone's home . . . ) |
| *à* | to / at / in |
| *en* | by / in |
| *quelquefois* | sometimes |
| *être* | to be |
| *c'est* | this is |
| *ce sont* | these are |
| *tu as perdu* | you've lost, you lost |
| *le livre* | the book |
| *la question* | the question |
| *sportif, -ve* | athletic |
| *l'Espagne* | Spain |
| *la Bretagne* | Brittany (a region in France) |
| *la Chine* | China |
| *l'Afrique* | Africa |
| *la Floride* | Florida |
| *l'Italie* | Italy |
| *les États-Unis* | the United States |

| *l'Amérique du Nord* | North America |
|---|---|
| *l'Europe* | Europe |

## PRACTICE EXERCISE 1

Fill in the blanks.

1. _____ or *ne pas être* (not to be), *c'est la question.*
2. *Les Etats–_____ sont en Amérique du Nord.*
3. *La Bretagne est en _____*
4. *Les étudiants de français ont des _____ de français.*
5. *Nous _____ chez mes parents.*
6. *Quelq_____ j'écoute la radio.*

## POINT 2: THE CONJUGATION OF THE VERB *ÊTRE*

The verb *être*, that is "to be," is a very useful verb. So, it's important to memorize the various forms of *être*, which would be the French equivalent of "am," "is," and "are." Do you remember back in Section 2 when you were introduced to regular –*er* verbs? You learned part of the conjugation – *la conjugaison* – of a verb like *danser: je danse*, and *tu danses*. Now we're going to look at the whole conjugation of *être* in the present tense. It's not that scary, but it certainly involves memorizing and practice. And now that you know the French pronouns (*je / tu / vous / il / elle / on / nous / vous / ils / elles*), we can jump right into *être*!

| *je suis* | I am |
|---|---|
| *tu es* | you are (familiar, of course) |
| *vous êtes* | you are (polite, as you know) |
| *il est* | he / it is (don't forget that *il* and *elle* can be things as well as people!) |
| *elle est* | she / it is |
| *on est* | one is / we are |
| *nous sommes* | we are |

| *vous êtes* | you are (plural polite or familiar) |
| *ils sont* | they are |
| *elles sont* | they are |

—*Je suis étudiante.*

—I am a student.

—*Tu es grand.*

—You are tall.

—*Vous êtes le maire.*

—You are the mayor.

—*Il est professeur.*

—He is a teacher.

—*Nous sommes frère et sœur.*

—We are brother and sister.

—*Vous êtes mes parents.*

—You are my parents.

—*Elles sont belles.*

—They are beautiful.

### PRACTICE EXERCISE 2

Fill in the blanks with the right form of *être*.

1. *Je _____ à Paris.*
2. *Il _____ à l'université.*
3. *Nous _____ chez Joséphine.*
4. *Tu _____ très gentille, Hélène !*
5. *Vous _____ le président ?*
6. *Elle _____ une très bonne amie.*
7. *On _____ au restaurant ce soir.*
8. *Elles _____ dans la chambre de Laura.*

## POINT 3: *LA LIAISON*

Do you remember the movie (or better yet, the book) Dangerous Liaisons? *Les Liaisons Dangeureuses*? In it, all sorts of people were, ahem, "linking" for various reasons. Well, there's a lot of linking, or *liaison*, in the French language, too. When you're talking about the language, *liaison* is when you link two words together in pronunciation. You carry over the sound at the end of word number 1, and you stick it onto the beginning of word number 2. Easy, right?

Like *l'élision*, where a small word like *je* or *le* loses its *e* before a vowel sound, *la liaison* makes French sound smoother. It happens between all sorts of words when the second word begins with a vowel sound.

For example, take the phrase *vous êtes*. You know that *vous* is pronounced [VOO] and *êtes* is pronounced [EHT], and that the –*s* of *vous* is normally silent. Say those two words together, and you have two clunky vowels rights next to each other, making French sound choppy and ugly. [VOO EHT.] But, if suddenly that silent –*s* at the end of *vous* were to wake up and be pronounced, stuck onto the beginning of the next word, you have [VOO ZEHT]. Much prettier! And much easier and smoother on the tongue. That's *liaison*.

With the verb *être*, there are a few cases of liaison:
*il est* is pronounced [ee-LAY]
*elle est* is pronounced [eh-LAY]
*on est* is pronounced [oh-NAY]
*vous êtes* is pronounced [voo ZEHT]

Notice that in the first two examples, the final –*l* of *il* and *elle* is always pronounced, but with liaison, you pronounce it as if it were the beginning of *est*. And in the last two examples, the final –*n* and the final –*s* are usually silent, but with liaison, they're pronounced as part of the next word.

Don't worry if this seems complicated. It'll get easier, and as long as you begin to train yourself to look out for it (when words begin with a vowel sound) you'll get it pretty quickly.

**PRACTICE EXERCISE 3**

Which of the following pairs of words would be connected by liaison? If so, which consonant is pronounced?

1. *étudiant français*     5. *chante bien*
2. *ils sont*              6. *vous adorez*
3. *elles aiment*         7. *nous regardons*
4. *je danse*             8. *nous aimons*

## POINT 4: *CHEZ*

*Chez* (at) is used with people's names and means "at someone's house". It's easy!
—*Tu es chez moi.*
—You're at my house.
—*Je suis chez mes parents.*
—I am at my parents'.
—*Ils sont chez Pierre.*
—They are at Pierre's.

**PRACTICE EXERCISE 4**

Answer the following questions using the cues provided.

1. *Mes amis sont chez moi ? (Oui.)*
2. *Il est chez Christelle ? (Oui.)*
3. *Vous êtes chez Jean ou chez Denis ? (Jean)*
4. *Nous sommes chez mes parents ? (Oui)*

**POINT 5:** *C'EST* AND *CE SONT*

*Ce* means "this" or "it," and *c'est* means "this is" or "it is." You use it when you're pointing to something (with words, at least.)

—*C'est moi !*

—It's me!

—*Qui est-ce ?*

—Who is it?

—*C'est mon ami.*

—This is my friend. / It's my friend.

*C'est* has a plural form: *ce sont*, which you can translate as "these are" or "they are."

—*Ce sont mes parents.*

—These are my parents.

—*Ce sont les livres que tu as perdus.*

—These are the books you've lost.

### PRACTICE EXERCISE 5

Fill in the blanks with *c'est* or *ce sont*.

1. _____ *mon ami.*

2. _____ *mon professeur.*

3. _____ *mes amis.*

4. _____ *la radio de Céline.*

5. _____ *mon bureau.*

6. _____ *mes sœurs.*

## POINT 6: THE USE OF ÊTRE

*Être* is used to describe an object or a person, to locate, to define, to identify . . . Just like "to be" in English, for the most part.

—*Je suis à Paris.*

—I am in Paris.

—*Tu es à l'université.*

—You are at the university.

—*Elle est grande.*

—She is tall.

—*Nous sommes étudiants.*

—We're students.

—*Vous êtes mes grands-parents.*

—You are my grandparents.

—*Ils sont aux États-Unis.*

—They are in the USA.

—*Nous sommes chez Paule.*

—We're at Paule's.

## POINT 7: THE LOCATION WORDS À, EN, AU, AND AUX

You may have noticed that French uses a few different location words (prepositions) depending on whether the location is a city or a country. Let's take a closer look.

1. Use *à* (in) in front of the name of a city or a town:

—*Il est à Boston.*

—He's in Boston.

—*Je suis à Los Angeles.*

—I am in Los Angeles.

2. Generally, use *en* (in) in front of the name of a country, a continent, or a state that is feminine in French. Yes, even the names of places are masculine or feminine in French. You can usually tell if a geographic name is feminine because it ends in –e. For example, *la France*, *l'Angleterre*, and *l'Espagne* are all feminine, but *le Canada* and *le Japon* are masculine. *Le Mexique* is an exception to this rule.

—*Il est en France, et vous êtes en Californie.*

—He's in France, and you're in California.

—*Ils sont en Europe.*

—They're in Europe.

Note that all nouns that end in -a in English will end in -e in French: *la Californie, la Floride, la Chine,* etc . . . Two exceptions are *le Canada* and *l'Angola.*

3. Use *au* or *aux* in front of masculine countries, continents and states. *Au* is singular, and *aux* is plural.

—*Tu es au Canada.*

—You are in Canada.

—*Vous êtes au Japon, et je suis aux États-Unis.*

—You are in Japan, and I'm in the United States.

( **WATCH THE DVD** )

That was quite a lot of information. So don't hesitate to review the section once or twice and then take a break and watch Section B, Part 3 on your DVD. That sounds relaxing, right?

# REVIEW EXERCISES

### REVIEW EXERCISE 1

Fill in the blanks with the correct form of *être*.

1. *Ce _____ mes livres.*
2. *Elle _____ sportive.*
3. *À l'université, on n' _____ pas paresseux.*
4. *Ils _____ perdus.*
5. *Vous _____ en Italie ?*
6. *Elles _____ chez mon ami.*
7. *Tu _____ ma sœur.*
8. *Je ne _____ pas malheureuse.*

### REVIEW EXERCISE 2

Choose *à, en, au, aux,* or *chez* in each of the following sentences.

1. *J'habite _____ New York.*
2. *Quelquefois, je vais _____ restaurant, _____ Momo.*
3. *Mon ami est _____ Afrique.*
4. *Mais il étudie _____ Etats-Unis, _____ New York University.*
5. *L'Italie et l'Espagne sont _____ Europe.*
6. *Toute la famille est _____ mes parents.*

### REVIEW EXERCISE 3

Please complete each sentence with one of these words:

*Marseille / grande / professeur / France / bleu / sportifs / moi / Chez Louis.*

1. *Les amis sont chez _____.*
2. *Je suis _____.*
3. *Mon oncle et ma tante sont _____.*
4. *Nous sommes à _____.*
5. *Mon oiseau est _____.*
6. *Ma chambre est _____.*

7. *L'Élysée est à Paris, en _____.*
8. *Nous sommes au restaurant _____.*

# Answer Key

**PRACTICE EXERCISE 1**
**1.** être **2.** Unis **3.** France **4.** livres **5.** sommes **6.** (Quelq)uefois

**PRACTICE EXERCISE 2**
**1.** suis **2.** est **3.** sommes **4.** es **5.** êtes **6.** est **7.** est **8.** sont

**PRACTICE EXERCISE 3**
**1.** Liaison – no **2.** Liaison – no **3.** Liaison – yes, -s is pronounced (as a z-)
**4.** Liaison – no **5.** Liaison – no **6.** Liaison – yes, -s is pronounced (as a z-)
**7.** Liaison – no **8.** Liaison – yes, -s is pronounced (as a z-)

**PRACTICE EXERCISE 4**
**1.** Oui, mes amis sont chez moi. **2.** Oui, il est chez Christelle. **3.** Vous êtes chez Jean. **4.** Oui, nous sommes chez mes parents.

**PRACTICE EXERCISE 5**
**1.** C'est **2.** C'est **3.** Ce sont **4.** C'est **5.** C'est **6.** Ce sont

**REVIEW EXERCISE 1**
**1.** sont **2.** est **3.** est **4.** sont **5.** êtes **6.** sont **7.** es **8.** suis

**REVIEW EXERCISE 2**
**1.** à **2.** au, Chez **3.** en **4.** aux, à **5.** en **6.** chez

**REVIEW EXERCISE 3**
**1.** moi **2.** professeur **3.** sportifs **4.** Marseille **5.** bleu **6.** grande **7.** France
**8.** Chez Louis

# Descriptive Adjectives

**POINT 1:** VOCABULARY

This list of vocabulary includes a lot of descriptive adjectives. Just as in previous vocabulary lists, you'll see both a masculine and a feminine form, as in *bleu, -e,* which means that *bleu* is masculine, and *bleue* is feminine. We'll come right back to what all of that means in this section. But first, here are the words.

| | |
|---|---|
| *bleu, -e* | blue |
| *long, -ue* | long |
| *cruel, -le* | cruel |
| *intellectuel, -le* | intellectual |
| *gros, -se* | big, fat |
| *actif, -ve* | active |
| *musclé, -e* | muscular, "buff" |
| *beau, belle* | beautiful |
| *court, -e* | short |
| *vieux, vieille* | old |
| *jeune* | young |
| *la robe* | the dress |
| *la chemise* | the shirt / blouse |

| | | |
|---|---|---|
| *le pantalon* | the pants | |
| *le manteau* | the coat | |

**PRACTICE EXERCISE 1**

Match the French words with their equivalents in English.

| | | |
|---|---|---|
| 1. | *sportif* | blue |
| 2. | *mince* | short |
| 3. | *verte* | happy |
| 4. | *gros* | thin |
| 5. | *belle* | active |
| 6. | *intellectuel* | muscular |
| 7. | *travailleur* | beautiful |
| 8. | *heureux* | kind |
| 9. | *petite* | lazy |
| 10. | *court* | hardworking |
| 11. | *grand* | green |
| 12. | *actif* | big |
| 13. | *musclé* | intellectual |
| 14. | *paresseux* | fat |
| 15. | *gentil* | little |
| 16. | *bleu* | athletic |

**POINT 2:** FRENCH ADJECTIVES AGREE WITH NOUNS

Adjectives are words that describe nouns or pronouns, like happy, big, lazy, smart, interesting, succulent, exceptional, punctilious . . . In English, adjectives are invariable, which means that they never change form, regardless of whether they're describing a man or a woman, or several men or several women.

But in French, adjectives change form depending on who or what they're describing. This is called "agreement." Adjectives in French agree with the noun or pronoun they describe, which means if a noun or pronoun is feminine singular, the adjective will be feminine singular, too, and if a noun or pronoun is masculine plural, the adjective will be masculine plural, too. Logical, isn't it? And actually, this isn't something totally new to you. You've been seeing adjectives used this way all along, since way back in the beginning when you saw *bonjour* and *bonne nuit*. *Bon* is masculine singular, and *bonne* is feminine singular.

The basic form of an adjective is its masculine singular form. Usually, to make it feminine singular, you just add an *–e*, unless the adjective already ends in *–e*, in which case you leave it alone. And to make an adjective plural, just add an *–s* to the appropriate singular form. So, you have, in the order masculine singular, feminine singular, masculine plural, feminine plural:

| | |
|---|---|
| *grand, grande, grands, grandes* | big |
| *bleu, bleue, bleus, bleues* | blue |
| *petit, petite, petits, petites* | little |
| *jeune, jeune, jeunes, jeunes* | young (Note that the basic form already ends in *–e*.) |

Here are some more examples:

—*L'oiseau est bleu. / Les oiseaux sont bleus.*
—The bird is blue. / The birds are blue.
—*Ma sœur est mince. / Mes sœurs sont minces.*
—My sister is thin. / My sisters are thin.
—*La fille est grande et le garçon est grand. / Les filles sont grandes et les garçons sont grands.*
—The girl is tall and the boy is tall. / The girls are tall and the boys are tall.

—*Le pantalon est court. / Les pantalons sont courts.*
—The pants are short. / The (several pairs of) pants are short.


**PRACTICE EXERCISE 2**

Choose the proper form of the adjective for each sentence.

1. *Les robes sont* _____ *(court, courte, courts, courtes.)*
2. *L'homme est* _____ *(grand, grande, grands, grandes.)*
3. *Le tapis est* _____ *(bleu, bleue, bleus, bleues).*
4. *La ville est* _____ *(beau, belle).*
5. *Le professeur est* _____ *(gros, grosse).*
6. *Les enfants sont parfois* _____ *(cruel, cruelle, cruels, cruelles) avec les animaux.*


## POINT 3: THE OTHER ADJECTIVES

You probably noticed that word "usually" when you read the last point about forming adjectives. As you can probably guess, there are a lot of adjectives that are irregular and that follow a pattern a little different from the regular ––, -e, -s, -es you've seen so far. Again, the only trick is . . . yes, you've got it . . . to M E M O R I Z E ! But don't worry; it's not as bad as it sounds. There are plenty of regular patterns that will help you. Very few forms come completely out of left field.


1. Adjectives ending in -el or -il will take an additional -le in the feminine, and an -s in the plural:
   *gentil: gentille, gentils, gentilles* – nice, kind
   *cruel: cruelle, cruels, cruelles* – cruel
   *intellectuel: intellectuelle, intellectuels, intellectuelles* – intellectual

2. Adjectives ending in -*f* will replace the -*f* with -*ve* in the feminine, and receive an -*s* in the plural:
*sportif: sportive, sportifs, sportives* – athletic
*actif: active, actifs, actives* – active

3. Adjectives ending in -*s* will double the –*s* and add an –*e* in the feminine, and then add an –*s* on top of that for the feminine plural. The masculine plural will look just like the masculine singular, since it already ends in –*s*:
*gros: grosse, gros, grosses* – big, fat

4. Adjectives ending in -*eux* or -*eur* will change to -*euse* in the feminine, and then just receive an extra -*s* in the feminine plural. The masculine plural for –*eux* adjectives will look just like the singular, but the –*eur* adjectives will add an –*s*:
*heureux: heureuse, heureux, heureuses* – happy
*travailleur: travailleuse, travailleurs, travailleuses* – hardworking

5. There are some oddballs, such as:
*bon: bonne, bons, bonnes* – good
*beau: belle, beaux, belles* – beautiful
*long: longue, longs, longues* – long
*vieux: vieille, vieux, vieilles* – old

Also note that in French, adjectives of nationality, such as *français* or *américain*, are not capitalized:
—*le cinéma français / la musique française*
—French movies / French music

## POINT 4: WHERE DOES THE ADJECTIVE GO?

You've probably noticed by now that the adjective in French usually comes after the noun that it describes, which is unlike English, where the adjective comes before the noun:

—*le professeur travailleur*

—the hardworking professor

—*la femme française*

—the French woman

—*les garçons intelligents*

—the intelligent boys

But there are a few common cases where the adjective comes before the noun, just like in English. The adjectives *petit* (small), *grand* (big, tall), *jeune* (young), *vieux* (old), *bon* (good), *mauvais* (bad), *beau* (beautiful), *joli* (pretty), *gentil* (kind), and *nouveau* (new) all come before the noun they describe.

—*le jeune garçon*

—the young boy

—*la vieille femme*

—the old woman

—*le nouveau livre*

—the new book

### PRACTICE EXERCISE 3

Choose the proper form of the adjective for each sentence.

1. *La robe est _____. (long, longue, longs, longues).*
2. *Mes amis sont très _____ (sportif, sportive, sportifs, sportives).*
3. *Mon chien est _____ (gentil, gentille, gentils, gentilles).*
4. *Carlos est _____ (heureux, heureuse, heureuses).*
5. *Natalie et Sylvie sont _____ (travailleur, travailleuse, travailleurs, travailleuses).*

6. *Les Etats-Unis sont* _____ *(grand, grande, grands, grandes).*

7. *Véronique, tu es toujours* _____ *(heureux, heureuse, heureuses).*

8. *L'université est* _____ *(vieux, vieille, vieilles).*

( **WATCH THE DVD** )

Again, if anything is unclear, you should review this section as many times as you'd like. When you're ready to move on, watch Section C, Part 3 on your DVD.

# *REVIEW EXERCISES*

### REVIEW EXERCISE 1

Complete each sentence by repeating the adjective in its correct form.

1. *Le tapis est bleu, et les fenêtres aussi sont* _____.

2. *L'homme est vieux, et les femmes aussi sont* _____.

3. *Ma mère est intelligente, et mes frères aussi sont* _____.

4. *Ton grand-père est gentil, et les filles aussi sont* _____.

5. *La nuit est longue, et le jour aussi est* _____.

6. *Elles sont heureuses, et il est* _____ *aussi.*

7. *Carlos et moi sommes sportifs, et ma sœur aussi est* _____.

8. *Les étudiants sont cruels, et le professeur aussi est* _____.

### REVIEW EXERCISE 2

Write the adjective in parentheses in the correct form.

1. *Les étudiantes à l'université sont* _____ *(travailleur).*

2. *Les vélos* _____ *(bleu) sont ici.*

3. *Les chambres sont très* _____ *(petit).*

4. *C'est une* _____ *(beau) ville !*

5. *Mes grands-parents sont* _____ *(vieux).*

6. *Les fenêtres de la chambre sont* _____ *(grand).*

### REVIEW EXERCISE 3

Choose the right answer.

1. The feminine plural form of *beau* is *belle, beaux,* or *belles*?
2. The masculine plural form of *longue* is *long, longs,* or *longue*?
3. *Jeune* is the same for masculine and feminine: *Vrai* ou *Faux*?
4. The masculine plural form of *gros* is *grosses, grosse,* or *gros*?
5. The feminine singular form of *travailleur* is *travailleurs* or *travailleuse*?
6. The masculine singular form of *vieux* is *vieux, vieilles,* or *vieille*?

### REVIEW EXERCISE 4

Translate each of the following sentences from English into French. Don't forget to watch out for those adjectives!

1. The old university is beautiful.
2. My friends are very athletic.
3. My grandparents are very active.
4. Here is a green plant.
5. My sister eats a lot but she is thin!
6. I like French movies. (movies = cinema)
7. The days are long.
8. My brother is not very tall.

# Answer Key

### PRACTICE EXERCISE 1

**1.** sportif – athletic  **2.** mince – thin  **3.** verte – green  **4.** gros – fat  **5.** belle – beautiful  **6.** intellectuel – intellectual  **7.** travailleur – hardworking  **8.** heureux – happy  **9.** petite – little  **10.** court – short  **11.** grand – big  **12.** actif – active  **13.** musclé – muscular  **14.** paresseux – lazy  **15.** gentil – kind  **16.** bleu – blue

**PRACTICE EXERCISE 2**

**1.** courtes **2.** grand **3.** bleu **4.** belle **5.** gros **6.** cruels

**PRACTICE EXERCISE 3**

**1.** longue **2.** sportifs **3.** gentil **4.** heureux **5.** travailleuses **6.** grands
**7.** heureuse **8.** vieille

**REVIEW EXERCISE 1**

**1.** bleues **2.** vieilles **3.** intelligents **4.** gentilles **5.** long **6.** heureux **7.** sportive
**8.** cruel

**REVIEW EXERCISE 2**

**1.** travailleuses **2.** bleus **3.** petites. **4.** belle **5.** vieux **6.** grandes

**REVIEW EXERCISE 3**

**1.** belles **2.** longs **3.** vrai **4.** gros **5.** travailleuse **6.** vieux

**REVIEW EXERCISE 4**

**1.** La vieille université est belle. **2.** Mes amis sont très sportifs. / Mes amies sont très sportives. **3.** Mes grands-parents sont très actifs. **4.** Voici une plante verte. **5.** Ma sœur mange beaucoup mais elle est mince ! **6.** J'aime le cinéma français. **7.** Les jours sont longs. **8.** Mon frère n'est pas très grand.

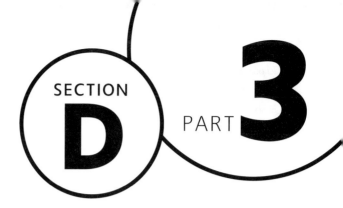

SECTION **D** PART **3**

# *Possessive Adjectives*

Possessive adjectives are adjectives that show possession, such as "my" or "your" or "her" in English. Since they're adjectives, they have to agree with the noun that they describe. In this section we'll cover all of that, but first, let's get a little more vocabulary under your belt.

**POINT 1:** VOCABULARY

| | |
|---|---|
| *ma, mon, mes* | my |
| *ta, ton, tes* | your (fam.) |
| *sa, son, ses* | her/his/its |
| *faire la sieste* | to take a nap |
| *le pompier* | the fireman |
| *le match de foot* | the soccer game |
| *faire du sport* | to play a sport |
| *le lit* | the bed |
| *le tapis* | the rug |
| *la lampe* | the lamp |
| *la table* | the table |
| *la chaise* | the chair |
| *le bureau* | the desk (also, office) |

| | |
|---|---|
| *la porte* | the door |
| *le crayon* | the pencil |
| *le stylo* | the pen |
| *la voiture* | the car |

**PRACTICE EXERCISE 1**

Match the French word or phrase on the left with its English equivalent.

| | | |
|---|---|---|
| 1. | *faire la sieste* | the bed |
| 2. | *la lampe* | the soccer game |
| 3. | *le tapis* | to take a nap |
| 4. | *le match de foot* | to do/play sports |
| 5. | *faire du sport* | the pen |
| 6. | *la voiture* | your |
| 7. | *le crayon* | the door |
| 8. | *le lit* | the lamp |
| 9. | *le stylo* | the car |
| 10. | *la chaise* | the chair |
| 11. | *la porte* | the pencil |
| 12. | *ton* | the rug |

**POINT 2: THE POSSESSIVE ADJECTIVES**

As you've seen, the possessive adjectives in English are: my, your, his, her, its, our, and their. French has pretty much the same possessive adjectives, but for now we're only going to cover "my," "your," "his," "her," and "its." The most important thing to realize about possessive adjectives in French is that they agree with the noun that they describe. For example, you saw in the vocabulary list that "my" can be *ma*, *mon*, or *mes* depending on what it describes.

—*C'est ma chambre.*

—This is my bedroom. (*Ma* is feminine singular because *chambre* is feminine singular. It doesn't matter if the speaker is a man or a woman.)

—*C'est mon livre.*

—This is my book. (*Mon* is masculine singular because *livre* is masculine singular.)

—*Ce sont mes amis.*

—These are my friends. (*Mes* is plural, either masculine or feminine, because *amis* is plural.)

As you can see, the possessive adjectives "my," "your," "his," "her," and "its" have three different forms – masculine singular, feminine singular, and plural – depending on whether the thing being possessed is masculine singular, feminine singular, or plural. Here's a chart that summarizes the forms. Can you see any patterns?

|  | *masculine/singular* | *feminine/singular* | *plural* |
|---|---|---|---|
| *my* | mon | ma | mes |
| *your* | ton | ta | tes |
| *his* | son | sa | ses |
| *her* | son | sa | ses |
| *its* | son | sa | ses |

Notice that *son/sa/ses* can mean "his," "her," or "its." But they don't follow the same pattern in French as they do in English. In English, the possessive adjectives change depending on the gender of the possessor – "his" for a masculine owner, "her" for a feminine owner, and "its" for an owner that is a thing. In French, though, the possessive adjectives follow the gender of the thing that's being possessed, regardless of who the owner is. So, *son* can mean "his" or "her" or "its," as long as the thing being possessed is masculine singular, such as *le livre* or *le stylo*. Here are a few more examples of possessive adjectives in French.

—*Son lit est dans la chambre.*

—His/Her bed is in the bedroom.

—*Sa voiture est blanche.*

—His/Her car is white.

—*Ses amis sont très gentils.*

—His/Her friends are very kind.

—*Mon livre est vert.*

—My book is green.

—*Ta maison est grande.*

—Your house is big.

—*J'aime tes CD !*

—I like your CD's!

—*Son université est à Paris.*

—Her/His university is in Paris.

Did you notice anything odd in that last example? *Université* is feminine, but the possessive adjective is the one that's usually reserved for masculine singular nouns – *son*, instead of *sa*. Can you guess why? Are you guessing that it has something to do with pronunciation? It's a bit like the elision; if a feminine noun begins with a vowel sound, *son*, *ton*, and *mon* are used instead of the normal *sa*, *ta*, and *ma*.

—*Mon amie est française.*

—My girlfriend is French.

—*Ton école n'est pas loin d'ici.*

—Your school is not far from here.

But if there's another word in between to break up the vowels, the regular feminine forms *ma*, *ta*, and *sa* are used.

—*Ma meilleure amie est française.*

—My best friend is French.

—*Ta nouvelle école n'est pas loin d'ici.*

—Your new school is not far from here.

## PRACTICE EXERCISE 2

Complete each sentence with the correct form of the possessive adjective given in English in parentheses.

1. *Ma sœur aime _____ chambre.* (my)
2. *Mon chien aime _____ ballon.* (his)
3. *J'adore _____ famille.* (your)
4. *Tu es gentil avec _____ grands-parents.* (your)
5. *Ce sont _____ fils et _____ fille?* (his) (his)
6. *Voilà _____ enfants !* (my)
7. *Je travaille à _____ école.* (her)
8. *Nous sommes avec _____ mari.* (her)

## PRACTICE EXERCISE 3

Choose from among the possessive adjectives to complete each sentence.

1. *C'est _____ maison. (ma mon mes)*
2. *Voici _____ sœur. (sa son ses)*
3. *C'est _____ chien ? (ta ton tes)*
4. *J'aime _____ amis. (ta ton tes)*
5. *Je mange chez _____ amie. (ma mon mes)*
6. *Ce sont _____ CD et _____ livres. (son sa ses)*

### ( WATCH THE DVD )

If you're ready to move on, now is the time to Watch Part 3, Section D, on your DVD.

# REVIEW EXERCISES

**REVIEW EXERCISE 1**

Choose the right form of the possessive adjective (given in the masculine singular form) for each of the following sentences.

1. *Voici (son) enfants.*
2. *Ils sont très gentils avec (mon) parents.*
3. *Tu aimes (son) grande chambre ?*
4. *Je préfère (mon) petite chambre.*
5. *(Son) amie est sportive et elle aime faire du sport.*
6. *(Ton) université est l'université de la Sorbonne à Paris.*
7. *(Son) ballon est bleu.*
8. *(Ton) parents sont grands et minces.*

**REVIEW EXERCISE 2**

Translate the following into French.

1. My university is big.
2. Your parents are kind.
3. Her sister is athletic.
4. But her brothers don't like to play sports.
5. My French books are old. (use: "books of French")
6. She likes her dog a lot.
7. Your family is very intellectual.
8. Your best friend is here!

# Answer Key

**PRACTICE EXERCISE 1**

**1.** faire la sieste – to take a nap  **2.** la lampe – the lamp  **3.** le tapis – the rug
**4.** le match de foot – the soccer game  **5.** faire du sport – to do/play sports

6. la voiture – the car **7.** le crayon – the pencil **8.** le lit – the bed **9.** le stylo – the pen **10.** la chaise – the chair **11.** la porte – the door **12.** ton – your

## PRACTICE EXERCISE 2
**1.** ma **2.** son **3.** ta **4.** tes **5.** son, sa **6.** mes **7.** son **8.** son

## PRACTICE EXERCISE 3
**1.** ma **2.** sa **3.** ton **4.** tes **5.** mon **6.** son/ses, ses

## REVIEW EXERCISE 1
**1.** ses **2.** mes **3.** sa **4.** ma **5.** Son **6.** Ton **7.** Son **8.** Tes

## REVIEW EXERCISE 2
**1.** Mon université est grande. **2.** Tes parents sont gentils. **3.** Sa sœur est sportive. **4.** Mais ses frères n'aiment pas faire du sport. **5.** Mes livres de français sont vieux. **6.** Elle aime beaucoup son chien. **7.** Ta famille est très intellectuelle. **8.** Ta meilleure amie est ici !

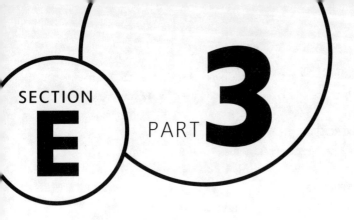

## *The Family*

**POINT 1:** VOCABULARY

| | |
|---|---|
| *comme* | like / as |
| *quand* | when |
| *les grands-parents* | the grandparents |
| *la grand-mère* | the grandmother |
| *le grand-père* | the grandfather |
| *la tante* | the aunt |
| *un / l'oncle* | an / the uncle |
| *le cousin* | the male cousin |
| *la cousine* | the female cousin |
| *le neveu* | the nephew |
| *la nièce* | the niece |
| *le mari* | the husband |
| *la femme* | the wife / the woman |
| *le fils* | the son |
| *la fille* | the daughter, the girl |
| *un / l'enfant* | a / the child |
| *un ordinateur* | a computer |
| *la fleur* | the flower |

| | |
|---|---|
| *un / l'oiseau* | a / the bird |
| *filer* | to leave quickly, to get out of somewhere quickly |

## PRACTICE EXERCISE 1

Match the French word or phrase on the left with the English equivalent on the right.

| | | |
|---|---|---|
| 1. | *mon oncle* | the computer |
| 2. | *la fleur* | the son |
| 3. | *comme ci, comme ça* | as / like |
| 4. | *je file* | the flower |
| 5. | *l'ordinateur* | the nephew |
| 6. | *quand* | the husband |
| 7. | *comme* | when |
| 8. | *sa tante* | my uncle |
| 9. | *le neveu* | a girl |
| 10. | *l'enfant* | my parents |
| 11. | *la fille* | the wife |
| 12. | *une fille* | her aunt |
| 13. | *le fils* | the child |
| 14. | *le mari* | the daughter |
| 15. | *la femme* | I'm leaving quickly |
| 16. | *mes parents* | so so |

## POINT 2: THE FAMILY TREE

You know how to say each of the following family members in French. Review this vocabulary until you're familiar with it, and then write down the names of the people in your family tree.

*les grands-parents :*

    *le grand-père*

    *la grand-mère*

*les petits-enfants* :
    *le petit-fils*
    *la petite-fille*
*les parents* :
    *le père*
    *la mère*
*les enfants* :
    *le fils*
    *la fille*
    *le frère*
    *la sœur*
*l'oncle*
*la tante*
*le neveu*
*la nièce*
*la cousine*
*le cousin*

Note that the articles here are pretty obvious, *le* for men and boys, *la* for women and girls.

**PRACTICE EXERCISE 2**
Complete the following sentences with the appropriate family vocabulary.

1. *Le frère de ma mère est mon* _____.
2. *La sœur de mon frère est ma* _____.
3. *Le mari de ma grand-mère est mon* _____.
4. *Le frère de mon cousin est mon* _____.
5. *La fille de mon oncle est ma* _____.
6. *Je suis l'* _____ *de mes parents.*

Way back in Part 2 you learned how to say "My name is . . ." *Je m'appelle . . .* You've also learned *il*, *elle*, and *tu*, so now let's put them together.

—*Tu t'appelles Georges.*

—Your name is Georges.

—*Il s'appelle Henri.*

—His name is Henry.

—*Elle s'appelle Sophie.*

—Her name is Sophie.

We won't get too much into the grammar behind this . . . yet! But for now, just notice that for *tu*, the verb ends in *–es*, and for *il* and *elle*, it just ends in *–e*. Also notice that there's a *t'* in the *tu* form, and a *s'* in the *il* and *elle* form.

### WATCH THE DVD

Ready for the DVD? If not, review this section in the book. But if you're all set to go on, watch Part 3, Section E of the DVD.

# REVIEW EXERCISES

### REVIEW EXERCISE 1

Replace the English words in parentheses with the appropriate French words. Don't forget to look for clues about gender, agreement, etc.

1. (I) *aime beaucoup les fleurs* (blue).
2. (You) *êtes* (my) *amis.*
3. (His) *ami est mon* (brother).
4. *Nous* (are) *heureux.*

5. *Mes* (grandparents) *sont* (active).
6. (Your) *grands oiseaux* (green) *sont très* (beautiful).
7. *Ils adorent marcher* (in) *Paris avec tes* (parents).
8. *Je* (am) (his) *amie*.

**REVIEW EXERCISE 2**

Translate each of the following sentences into English.

1. *Chez mes parents, les fleurs sont belles.*
2. *Il s'appelle Sébastien, comme moi.*
3. *Marcher dans les rues de Paris est super.*
4. *Le mari de ma sœur est grand.*
5. *Ça va comme ci, comme ça.*
6. *Mon ami aime faire beaucoup de sports.*
7. *Mon frère est mince, comme moi.*
8. *Mon oncle et ma tante sont Robert et Michelle.*

# *Answer Key*

**PRACTICE EXERCISE 1**

**1.** mon oncle – my uncle **2.** la fleur – the flower **3.** comme ci, comme ça – so so **4.** je file – I leave quickly **5.** l'ordinateur – the computer **6.** quand – when **7.** comme – as / like **8.** sa tante – her aunt **9.** le neveu – the nephew **10.** l'enfant – the child **11.** la fille – the daughter **12.** une fille – a girl **13.** le fils – the son **14.** le mari – the husband **15.** la femme – the wife **16.** mes parents – my parents

**PRACTICE EXERCISE 2**

**1.** oncle **2.** sœur **3.** grand-père **4.** cousin. **5.** cousine **6.** enfant

## REVIEW EXERCISE 1

**1.** J'aime beaucoup les fleurs bleues.  **2.** Vous êtes mes amis.  **3.** Son ami est mon frère.  **4.** Nous sommes heureux.  **5.** Mes grands-parents sont actifs.  **6.** Tes grands oiseaux verts sont très beaux.  **7.** Ils adorent marcher dans Paris avec tes parents.  **8.** Je suis son amie.

## REVIEW EXERCISE 2

**1.** At my parents', the flowers are beautiful.  **2.** His name is Sebastian, like me.  **3.** To walk in the streets of Paris is great. / Walking the streets of Paris is great.  **4.** My sister's husband is tall.  **5.** (It goes) so so.  **6.** My friend likes to do / play a lot of sports.  **7.** My brother is thin, like me.  **8.** My uncle and my aunt are Robert and Michelle.

# Mes Possessions

PART

4

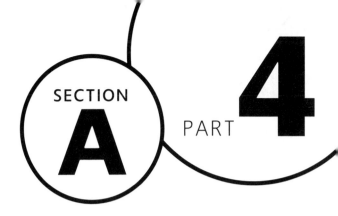

# Colors

You can probably guess that the name of Part 4, *Mes Possessions*, means "my possessions." In this part, you'll learn how to talk about what you have, to say what color something is, and to use the other articles and possessive adjectives . . . Not bad, huh? But first, as an appetizer, *voici* some new *vocabulaire*.

## POINT 1: VOCABULARY

This may look like a long vocabulary list, but don't worry. You've seen some of these words before, and you'll recognize what a lot of the new ones mean because they're cognates. Ready?

| | |
|---|---|
| *c'est* | it is / this is |
| *ce sont* | they are / these are |
| *c'est tout* | that's all |
| *n'est-ce pas?* | isn't it? |
| *il y a* | there is / there are |
| *aussi* | also |
| *midi* | noon |
| *minuit* | midnight |
| *bienvenue* | welcome |

| | |
|---|---|
| *s'appeler* | to be called, (one's) name is . . . |
| *habiter à* | to live in |
| *posséder* | to own |
| *la possession* | possession |
| *la maison* | the house |
| *la pièce* | the room |
| *la cuisine* | the kitchen |
| *la chaise* | the chair |
| *la table* | the table |
| *la porte* | the door |
| *un, l'appareil photo* | a, the camera |
| *la photo* | the picture / photograph |
| *une affiche* | a poster |
| *le basketball* | basket ball |
| *le courrier* | the mail |
| *un animal* | an animal/pet |
| *le chat* | the cat |
| *un oiseau* | a bird |
| *le poisson* | the fish |
| *le pain* | the bread |
| *personne* | nobody |
| *quelqu'un* | somebody / anybody |
| *rien* | nothing |
| *quelque chose* | something / anything |
| *un homme* | a man |
| *la femme* | the woman |
| *le garçon* | the boy |
| *la fille* | the girl |
| *un enfant* | a child |
| *le bébé* | the baby |
| *un arc-en-ciel* | a rainbow |
| *la couleur* | the color |

| | |
|---|---|
| *rouge* | red |
| *jaune* | yellow |
| *orange* | orange |
| *rose* | pink |
| *bleu* | blue |
| *vert* | green |
| *brun* | brown (as in hair, skin, or leather) |
| *marron* | brown (as in otherr things—books, houses, itc.) |
| *gris* | gray |
| *noir* | black |
| *violet, violette* | purple (masc., fem.) |
| *blanc, blanche* | white (masc., fem.) |

## PRACTICE EXERCISE 1

Is it *le ou la ou l'* ? Complete each sentence with the right article.

1. *J'aime manger _____ pain chaud.*

2. *_____ oiseau bleu est à moi.*

3. *_____ fille et _____ garçon vont dans _____ maison blanche.*

4. *Il y a _____ vélo de ma sœur.*

5. *_____ chat s'appelle Mak.*

6. *C'est _____ cadeau de mes parents !*

7. *_____ cuisine est grande.*

8. *Voici _____ courrier.*

9. *_____ photo en noir et blanc est dans sa chambre.*

10. *_____ femme et _____ homme mangent au restaurant.*

**POINT 2:** LES COULEURS

You saw a few colors in earlier lessons. Now let's look at all of them together:

*vert, bleu, violet, rose, rouge, orange, jaune, brun, marron, noir, gris, blanc . . .*

Now, that's a pretty *arc-en-ciel* (rainbow.) Note that the colors are adjectives, which means that they agree in gender and number with the nouns they describe. Their basic forms above are masculine. For the feminine, you usually add *-e* (unless the color already ends in *-e*), and for the plural, you add *-s*. For instance:

*le ciel bleu* / the blue sky (masculine / singular)
*la table verte* / the green table (feminine / singular)
*les vélos rouges* / the red bikes (masculine / plural)
*les maisons grises* / the gray houses (feminine / plural)

However, some of the feminine forms are a bit twisted. For example, *blanc* becomes *blanche*. It ends in a [-SH] sound instead of the nasal [–ah*n.] And *violet* becomes *violette*, with a double *t*.

—*le vélo blanc et la voiture blanche*
—the white bike and the white car
—*le tapis violet et la fleur violette*
—the purple rug and the purple flower

And *marron* and *orange* don't change at all.

—*le pantalon marron et la chaise marron*
—the brown pants and the brown chair

—*le livre orange et la fleur orange*

—the orange book and the orange flower

## PRACTICE EXERCISE 2

Connect the nouns in the first column with their most likely color. Use the endings on the colors as clues! See, grammar can be helpful!

| | | |
|---|---|---|
| 1. | *les poissons* | *bleus* |
| 2. | *les chats* | *blanc* |
| 3. | *le pain* | *jaune* |
| 4. | *la rose* | *rouges* |
| 5. | *les plantes* | *noirs* |
| 6. | *le ciel* | *rose* |
| 7. | *la table en bois* (wooden) | *orange* |
| 8. | *l'orange* | *vertes* |
| 9. | *le soleil* | *marron* |
| 10. | *les océans* | *gris* |

**POINT 3:** IL Y A . . .

Now this is one of those cases when French is easier than English. In English, at least if you want to speak grammatically correctly, you have to say "there is" for singular things and "there are" for plural things. There is one cat on the bed, but there are two cats on the floor. In French, all you need to know is *il y a*, in all cases.

—*Il y a deux plantes vertes dans la chambre de Pierre.*

—There are two green plants in Pierre's bedroom.

—*Il y a un croissant sur la table de la cuisine.*

—There is one croissant on the kitchen table.

You can also ask all sorts of useful questions with *il y a.*

—*Qu'est-ce qu' il y a ?*
—What's the matter? / What's wrong? / What do you want?
—*Est-ce qu' il y a autre chose ?*
—Is there anything else?
—*Est-ce qu'il y a du courrier pour moi ?*
—Is there any mail for me?

You also can use *il y a* with a negative like "nobody" or "nothing." Just don't forget to add *n'* before it.

—*Il n' y a personne ici.*
—There is no one here.
—*Il n' y a rien.*
—There is nothing.

**PRACTICE EXERCISE 3**
Rewrite these sentences, putting the words in the right order:
1. *un / dans / garage / Il / chat / y / le / a .*
2. *des / sur / Il / table / a / fleurs / y / la / aussi .*
3. *il / Est-ce / y / quelqu'un / a / qu' ?*
4. *Non, / a / n' / rien / il / y .*
5. *a / il / Qu' / y /est-ce / qu' ?*
6. *des / cuisine / Il / la / croissants / y / dans / a .*
7. *Il / de / pain / a / plus / n' y .*
8. *courrier / pour / qu' il / Est-ce / y / du / moi / a ?*

( **WATCH THE DVD** )

Ready for the DVD? If you are, go ahead and watch Part 4, Section A.

# REVIEW EXERCISES

### REVIEW EXERCISE 1

Translate each of the following words or phrases into French.

1. the fish
2. a bird
3. the man and the woman
4. a poster
5. the tables and the chairs
6. the red door
7. the blue bird
8. the black cat

### REVIEW EXERCISE 2

Find the right forms of the color adjectives in the following sentences.

1. *Voici des fleurs (blanc).*
2. *Tu préfères une table (bleu) ou (orange) ?*
3. *Ton courrier est dans la voiture (marron).*
4. *Les tapis (rouge) sont beaux.*
5. *Dans la chambre (vert), il y a beaucoup de plantes.*
6. *C'est ta chemise (violet) ?*
7. *Le ciel est souvent (gris) ici.*
8. *Il y a des robes (jaune), (rouge), (noir) et (rose).*

### REVIEW EXERCISE 3

Now translate these sentences into French.

1. There is a beautiful red rose on the table. (Remember that *belle* comes before the noun!)
2. Are there any croissants? (Use *des* for "any.")
3. There are also some yellow and orange balls in the garage. (Use *des* for "some.")

4. But what is the matter?
5. There's nothing.
6. There is no one in my house. (Use *chez moi* for "in my house.")
7. They are three white cars.
8. Here is your mail.
9. There is a pretty purple dress here. (Use *jolie* for "pretty," and don't forget where it goesl)
10. There are six doors. They are black.

# Answer Key

**PRACTICE EXERCISE 1**
**1.** le  **2.** L'  **3.** La, le, la  **4.** le  **5.** Le  **6.** le  **7.** La.  **8.** le  **9.** La  **10.** La, l'

**PRACTICE EXERCISE 2**
**1.** les poissons rouges  **2.** les chats noirs  **3.** le pain blanc  **4.** la rose rose  **5.** les plantes vertes  **6.** le ciel gris  **7.** la table marron  **8.** l'orange orange  **9.** le soleil jaune  **10.** les océans bleus

**PRACTICE EXERCISE 3**
**1.** Il y a un chat dans le garage.  **2.** Il y a aussi des fleurs sur la table.  **3.** Est-ce qu'il a y quelqu'un ?  **4.** Non, il n' y a rien.  **5.** Qu' est-ce qu' il y a ?  **6.** Il y a des croissants dans la cuisine.  **7.** Il n' y a plus de pain.  **8.** Est-ce qu' il y a du courrier pour moi ?

**REVIEW EXERCISE 1**
**1.** le poisson (or les poissons)  **2.** un oiseau  **3.** l'homme et la femme  **4.** une affiche  **5.** les tables et les chaises  **6.** la porte rouge  **7.** l'oiseau bleu  **8.** le chat noir

## REVIEW EXERCISE 2

**1.** blanches **2.** bleue, orange **3.** marron **4.** rouges **5.** verte **6.** violette **7.** gris **8.** jaunes, rouges, noires, roses.

## REVIEW EXERCISE 3

**1.** Il y a une belle rose rouge sur la table. **2.** Est-ce qu'il y a des croissants ? **3.** Il y a des ballons jaunes et orange dans le garage. **4.** Mais qu'est-ce qu'il y a ? **5.** Il n'y a rien. **6.** Il n'y a personne chez moi. **7.** Il y a trois voitures blanches. **8.** Voici ton courrier. **9.** Il y a une jolie robe violette ici. **10.** Il y a six portes. Elles sont noires.

## *The Verb* AVOIR

First there was to be (*être*) or not to be. And now, there's to have (*avoir*) or not to have. But to have what? More vocabulary, of course!

**POINT 1:** VOCABULARY

| | |
|---|---|
| *notre, nos* | our |
| *votre, vos* | your (polite or plural) |
| *leur, leurs* | their |
| *moi* | me |
| *toi* | you |
| *lui* | him |
| *elle* | her |
| *la chose* | the thing |
| *le garage* | the garage |
| *la voiture* | the car |
| *le vélo* | the bike |
| *le cadeau* | the present |
| *le croissant* | the croissant |
| *le sandwich* | the sandwich |
| *le cerveau* | the brain |

| | |
|---|---|
| *le message* | the message |
| *pratique* | practical |
| *au travail* | at work |
| *pour* | for |

## PRACTICE EXERCISE 1

Fill in the blanks with an appropriate word from your vocabulary supply. You'll see some clues to help you along the way.

1. *La table, la voiture, la télé sont des c_____.*
2. *Avoir une v_____est pratique.*
3. *Le _____c'est comme la bicyclette.*
4. *Les voitures sont dans le _____.*
5. In French, there is a saying: *"moi, c'est moi, et _____, c'est toi".*
6. *À midi, au travail, je mange un _____.*
7. A favorite French pastry is *le _____.*
8. *Les enfants sont à l'école et les parents au t_____.*

## POINT 2: THE VERB *AVOIR*

We've already learned one really, really important verb: *être*, to be. And, as you remember, it's an irregular verb. Which means that you had to memorize all of its irregular forms. Here they are again:

| | |
|---|---|
| *je suis* | I am |
| *tu es* | you are |
| *il / elle / on est* | he / she / it / one is |
| *nous sommes* | we are |
| *vous êtes* | you are |
| *ils / elles sont* | they are |

Good! Now, guess what. There's another really, really important verb that we're going to sink our teeth into, and that is . . . *avoir*, to have. And, yes, it's irregular. But conjugations speak louder than explanations, so here are the forms of *avoir*. Keep an eye out for similarities it has with your other irregular friend, *être*.

| | |
|---|---|
| *j'ai* | I have |
| *tu as* | you have |
| *il / elle / on a* | he / she / it / one has |
| *nous avons* | we have |
| *vous avez* | you have |
| *ils /elles ont* | they have |

Did you notice the similarities? For example, *tu es* and *tu as*, or *ils ont* and *ils sont*. These patterns can make the forms easier to remember, but also easier to confuse. That's why it's important to memorize each verb and its forms as they come.

And . . . don't forget your *liaisons dangeureuses*! You've got *liaisons* to link pronunciation between, for example, *on* and *a*, or, *ils* and *ont*.

—*Elles ont* [ehl-zoh*n] *des messages.*

—They have some messages.

—*Ils sont* [eel-soh*n] *dans la cuisine.*

—They are in the kitchen.

Don't forget your rules on how to pronounce S in French. If there's one S, it's got the Z sound, but if there are two SS, or one S at the beginning of a word, it's got the S sound. So, you'll say *possessions* and *soleil* both with a regular S sound as in Sam. But *rose*, both the flower and the color, has a soft Z sound as in Zachary.

### PRACTICE EXERCISE 2

Let's get back to *avoir*. Connect each of the following subjects with the correct form of *avoir*.

1. *j'*            *ont*
2. *nous*          *a*
3. *le garçon*     *ont*
4. *ils*           *a*
5. *Marie et Stéphanie*   *ai*
6. *tu*            *avons*
7. *le chat*       *a*
8. *toi et moi, nous*   *avez*
9. *on*            *avons*
10. *vous*          *as*

## POINT 3: THE USES OF *AVOIR*

1. The verb *avoir* can be used to talk about what you possess, just like the verb "to have." For example, read the following passage:

   —*Je m'appelle Antoine. J'habite à Buffalo avec ma mère et mes frères. J'ai un chat, ma mère a un oiseau et mes frères ont un chien.*

   —My name is Antoine. I live in Buffalo with my mother and my brothers. I have a cat, my mother has a bird, and my brothers have a dog.

   As you can see, the use of *avoir* is easy once you've memorized its forms. Here are some other examples:

   —*Nous avons des amis à Paris.*

   —We have some friends in Paris.

   —*Mon frère et sa femme ont une grande maison.*

   —My brother and his wife have a big house.

   —*Vous avez du pain ?*

   —Do you have any bread?

But with *avoir*, you can express much more than possession. There are a lot of expressions in French that use *avoir* where you would use "to be" in English.

*avoir faim* – to be hungry
—*Nous sommes au restaurant et nous avons faim !*
—We're at the restaurant and we're hungry!

*avoir soif* – to be thirsty
—*Nous avons très soif.*
—We are very thirsty.

*avoir froid* – to be cold
—*Au Canada, j'ai toujours froid.*
—In Canada, I am always cold.

*avoir chaud* – to be hot/warm
—*En Espagne, j'ai chaud.*
—In Spain, I'm hot.

*avoir sommeil* – to be sleepy
—*Les enfants ont sommeil.*
—The children are sleepy.

*avoir peur* – to be afraid
—*Ta petite sœur a peur de mon chien.*
—Your little sister is afraid of my dog.

*avoir raison* – to be right
—*J'ai toujours raison !*
—I'm always right!

*avoir tort* – to be wrong

—*Et toi, tu as tort !*

—And you are wrong!

Pretty impressive, huh? And there's more. In French, you use *avoir* to say how old you are, again, where English uses the verb "to be."

—*Quel âge as-tu ?*

—How old are you?

—*J'ai vingt ans.*

—I'm twenty years old.

—*Non, je n'ai plus seize ans.*

—No, I'm no longer sixteen.

—*Vous avez trente-huit ans ?*

—You're thirty eight?

And of course, you remember the expression *il y a* (there is / there are.) That little *a* is actually the *il* form of *avoir*. So, literally, *il y a* means something like "it has there . . . "

—*Il y a des enfants à l'école.*

—There are some children at the school.

—*Il y a aussi un professeur.*

—There is also a teacher.

A good way to review everything you've just learned is to go over it a couple of more times, and then read the paragraph below:

—*Salut, c'est encore Patrick. J'ai dix-huit ans. J'ai faim ! Et Valérie et Hélène ont faim aussi, parce qu'il est midi. Nous avons soif aussi.*

—Hi, it's Patrick again. I'm 18 years old. I'm hungry! Et Valérie and Hélène are hungry, too, because it's noon. We're also thirsty.

Did you think we would have just forgotten about numbers? Of course not . . . And since you just learned how to say how old you are, it's a good idea to cover those numbers. And maybe you want to say how many of something *tu as*, since this is such a material world.

0 *zéro*

| | |
|---|---|
| 1 *un* (masculine) | 11 *onze* |
| *une* (feminine) | |
| 2 *deux* | 12 *douze* |
| 3 *trois* | 13 *treize* |
| 4 *quatre* | 14 *quatorze* |
| 5 *cinq* | 15 *quinze* |
| 6 *six* | 16 *seize* |
| 7 *sept* | 17 *dix-sept* |
| 8 *huit* | 18 *dix-huit* |
| 9 *neuf* | 19 *dix-neuf* |
| 10 *dix* | 20 *vingt* |
| | 21 *vingt et un* |

There are just a few things to point out about the numbers. One is the only number that has both a feminine and a masculine form, *une* (fem.) and *un* (masc.).

—*J'ai un vélo et une voiture.*

—I have one bicycle and one car. / I have a bike and a car.

You have to pronounce the last letters of *cinq*, *six*, *sept*, *huit*, and *dix* when counting or saying the date. They sound a bit like: sank, seess, seht, weet, and deess. But when you use them in a sentence, you only slightly pronounce the last consonants of *cinq* and *sept*, and you don't pronounce the last consonants of *six*, *huit*, and *dix* at all.

—*Elle a cinq livres.* (*Cinq* sounds like [san(k)].)

—She has five books.


—*Elle a sept frères.* (*Sept* sounds like [seh(t)].)

—She has seven brothers.

—*J'ai six chats.* (*Six* sounds like [see].)

—I have six cats.


But of course, if there's *liaison*, you do pronounce those last consonants.

—*Elle a <u>huit ans</u>.* [wee tah*n]

—She's eight years old.

—*Nous avons <u>dix amis</u> chez nous.* [dee zah-mee]

—We have ten friends at home.


## PRACTICE EXERCISE 3

Write each of the following numbers in French.

1. one
2. nine
3. fourteen
4. sixteen
5. twenty
6. twelve
7. seven
8. four
9. six
10. fifteen
11. eighteen
12. three


**WATCH THE DVD**

Bravo! Now, you may want to go over Part 4, Section B again, and then, watch your DVD.

# REVIEW EXERCISES

### REVIEW EXERCISE 1

Complete each sentence with the right form of *avoir*.

1. *J'_____ froid aussi.*
2. *Quel âge _____ ton frère et ta sœur ?*
3. *Ils _____ dix-huit et vingt ans.*
4. *Les enfants _____ peur du chien.*
5. *Mais qu'est-ce qu'il _____ ?*
6. *On _____ toujours raison.*
7. *Ils mangent du pain parce qu'ils _____ faim.*
8. *Nous _____ une maison à Paris, mais nous habitons à Boston*
9. *Tu _____ ces trois films en DVD ?*
10. *Vous _____ une voiture noire.*

### REVIEW EXERCISE 2

For each sentence, choose the right word from the three choices in parenthesis:

1. *Il y (ont – est – a) quatre chaises vertes dans la cuisine.*
2. *Vous (êtes – avez – as) faim ? Voici des croissants.*
3. *Il y a (une – un – deux) pièce dans un studio.*
4. *Ils (sont – ont – avons) froid.*
5. *Tu (es – a – as) vingt et un ans ?*
6. *Nous (avons – sommes – avez) dix étudiants français.*
7. *J' (as – a – ai) très sommeil.*
8. *Les carottes sont (jaunes – rouges – orange).*
9. *Elle a peur des chats (noir – noires – noirs).*
10. *Les fleurs (blancs – blanches – blanche) sont belles.*

Write the numbers in parentheses.

1.  *J'ai (1) chien.*
2.  *Nous mangeons (3) sandwichs.*
3.  *Elle est à Boston pour (21) jours.*
4.  *Sa sœur a (18) ans.*
5.  *(10), c'est (5) et (5).*
6.  *C'est l'exercice (13) !*

### REVIEW EXERCISE 4

Translate the following sentences:

1.  I'm at work and I'm cold.
2.  My brother's dog is hungry.
3.  They have three cars. They are in the garage.
4.  Are there any croissants in the kitchen? (Start with: *Est-ce qu'il y a des . . .*)
5.  You're wrong, he's sixteen. (Use the formal.)
6.  There are a lot of things in my bedroom. (A lot of is: *beaucoup de.*)
7.  She is not afraid.
8.  We are hot and very thirsty! (Use *on.*)

# *Answer Key*

### PRACTICE EXERCISE 1

**1.** choses  **2.** voiture  **3.** vélo  **4.** garage  **5.** toi  **6.** sandwich  **7.** croissant
**8.** travail

### PRACTICE EXERCISE 2

**1.** j' – ai  **2.** nous – avons  **3.** le garçon – a  **4.** ils – ont  **5.** Marie et Stéphanie –
ont  **6.** tu – as  **7.** le chat – a  **8.** toi et moi, nous – avons  **9.** on – a  **10.** vous –
avez

**PRACTICE EXERCISE 3**

**1.** un / une  **2.** neuf  **3.** quatorze  **4.** seize  **5.** vingt  **6.** douze  **7.** sept  **8.** quatre
**9.** six  **10.** quinze  **11.** dix-huit  **12.** trois

**REVIEW EXERCISE 1**

**1.** ai  **2.** ont  **3.** ont  **4.** ont  **5.** a  **6.** a  **7.** ont  **8.** avons  **9.** as  **10.** avez

**REVIEW EXERCISE 2**

**1.** a  **2.** avez  **3.** une  **4.** ont  **5.** as  **6.** sommes  **7.** ai  **8.** orange  **9.** noirs
**10.** blanches

**REVIEW EXERCISE 3**

**1.** un  **2.** trois  **3.** vingt et un  **4.** dix-huit  **5.** Dix, cinq, cinq  **6.** treize

**REVIEW EXERCISE 4**

**1.** Je suis au travail et j'ai froid.  **2.** Le chien de mon frère a faim.  **3.** Ils ont trois
voitures. Elles sont dans le garage.  **4.** Est-ce qu'il y a des croissants dans la
cuisine ?  **5.** Vous avez tort, il a seize ans.  **6.** Il y a beaucoup de choses dans
ma chambre.  **7.** Elle n'a pas peur.  **8.** On a chaud et très soif !

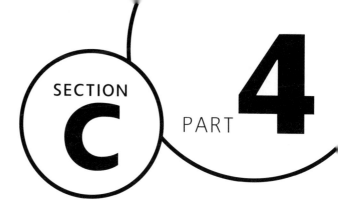

# Indefinite Articles

Now we'll get to the indefinite articles, which correspond to "a" or "an" or "some" instead of "the." But first, let's add some vocabulary to the mix.

## POINT 1: VOCABULARY

| | |
|---|---|
| *un, une* | a, an |
| *des* | some, any |
| *la pomme de terre* | the potato |
| *la carotte* | the carrot |
| *le sac* | the bag |
| *la table de la cuisine* | the kitchen table |
| *le bureau* | the desk, the office |
| *le stylo* | the pen |
| *le crayon* | the pencil |
| *le cahier* | the notebook |
| *le message* | the message |
| *le travail* | the work, job |
| *l'anniversaire* | the birthday |

**PRACTICE EXERCISE 1**

Match the French word or expression on the right with its English equivalent on the left.

| | | |
|---|---|---|
| 1. | *la chaise* | the notebook |
| 2. | *des* | a |
| 3. | *le stylo* | the bag |
| 4. | *la pomme de terre* | the table |
| 5. | *le crayon* | the pen |
| 6. | *le bureau* | the potato |
| 7. | *le cahier* | the pencil |
| 8. | *une, un* | the desk |
| 9. | *la table* | any |
| 10. | *le sac* | the carrot |
| 11. | *le message* | the chair |
| 12. | *la carotte* | the message |

**POINT 2:** *UN, UNE, DES*: **THE INDEFINITE ARTICLES**

As you read right before diving into some new vocabulary, the indefinite articles in English are "a," "an," and "some." They're called indefinite, because they're, well, indefinite. Think about it. When you say "the book" you're talking about a definite, specific book. But when you say "a book" or "some books," any old book will do. You're being indefinite.

In French, the indefinite articles are *un* for masculine nouns, *une* for feminine nouns, and *des* for plurals, either masculine or feminine.
—*un ordinateur, des CD, un livre, une maison, des stylos, une table*
—a computer, some CD's, a book, a house, some pens, a table

Easy, right? So you know that the article always agrees with the gender and number of the noun, and you know which articles are which, so all you need to know is when to use l'article indéfini.

You use the indefinite article when referring to general things (versus particular ones). It's pretty much like English.

—J'ai un crayon.
—I have a pencil.
—J'ai une robe bleue aussi.
—I have a blue dress too.
—Nous avons des stylos noirs.
—We have some black pens.
—Il y a des fleurs blanches ?
—Are there any white flowers?
—As-tu des crayons de couleur?
—Do you have any color pencils?

Notice in the last three examples that the plural indefinite article in English, "some," changes to "any" in questions. In French, it stays the same – des. There are also plenty of cases in English when you don't use "the" or "some" or "a" in front of nouns – the nouns stay naked, so to speak. French doesn't like this very much, though, so it's always clothing nouns.

—There are books on the table.
—Il y a des livres sur la table.
—Birds sing.
—Les oiseaux chantent.

Don't worry about the rules for this just yet. For now, just expect to see French articles in a lot of places that you might think sound a bit odd. Remember – just because it sounds odd in one language, it doesn't necessarily sound odd in another!

## PRACTICE EXERCISE 2

Let's practice. Fill in the blanks with the right indefinite article.

1. Vous avez _____ frères et _____ sœurs aussi.

2. As-tu _____ radio ou _____ stéréo ?

3. Nous avons _____ animaux.

4. Ma mère a _____ croissants et _____ pain dans son sac.

5. Mes amis ont _____ travail intéressant.

6. Mon amie possède _____ livres anciens.

7. J'ai _____ beau cadeau pour toi !

8. Tu préfères _____ plante verte ou _____ fleurs jaunes ?

9. C'est _____ appareil photo.

10. "_____ homme et _____ femme" est _____ film français.

---

( **WATCH THE DVD** )

If you're ready to move on, go to Part 4, Section C of your DVD for some more on these indefinite articles. And then come back for your review exercises.

# REVIEW EXERCISES

## REVIEW EXERCISE 1

Write the correct article for each of the following. First, write the definite, and then the indefinite. For example, if you see: _____ ordinateur; _____ ordinateur, you'd write *l'* and then *un*.

1. _____ enfants; _____ enfants

2. _____ fleur rose; _____ fleur rose

3. _____ vélo rouge; _____ vélo rouge

4. _____ cinémas; _____ cinémas

5. _____ femmes; _____ femmes

6. _____ université; _____ université
7. _____ stylo noir; _____ stylo noir
8. _____ cahier marron; _____ cahier marron
9. _____ chambre verte; _____ chambre verte
10. _____ livres jaunes; _____ livres jaunes

### REVIEW EXERCISE 2

Change each of these phrases to the plural.

1. un sac de pommes de terre.
2. un bureau en bois marron.
3. un cahier et un crayon.
4. une table de cuisine.
5. un message.
6. une carotte.
7. un bon anniversaire.
8. une chaise bleue.

### REVIEW EXERCISE 3

Translate each of these sentences into English.

1. Il y a des pommes de terre et des carottes sur la table dans la cuisine.
2. Est-ce que vous avez faim ? Il y a un croissant dans le sac.
3. Au travail, il y a beaucoup de livres sur mon bureau.
4. Il y a aussi des stylos, des crayons et des cahiers.
5. Vous préférez des fleurs blanches ou une plante verte ?
6. C'est un cadeau pour votre anniversaire.

# Answer Key

### PRACTICE EXERCISE 1

**1.** la chaise – the chair **2.** des – any **3.** le stylo – the pen **4.** la pomme de terre
– the potato **5.** le crayon – the pencil **6.** le bureau – the desk **7.** le cahier –

the notebook **8.** une, un – a **9.** la table – the table **10.** le sac – the bag **11.** le message – the message **12.** la carotte – the carrot

## PRACTICE EXERCISE 2
**1.** des, des **2.** une, une **3.** des **4.** des, un **5.** un **6.** des **7.** un **8.** une, des **9.** un **10.** Un, une, un

## REVIEW EXERCISE 1
**1.** les enfants; des enfants **2.** la fleur rose; une fleur rose **3.** le vélo rouge; un vélo rouge **4.** les cinémas; des cinémas **5.** les femmes; des femmes **6.** l'université; une université **7.** le stylo noir; un stylo noir **8.** le cahier marron; un cahier marron **9.** la chambre verte; une chambre verte **10.** les livres jaunes; des livres jaunes

## REVIEW EXERCISE 2
**1.** des sacs de pommes de terre. **2.** des bureaux en bois marron. **3.** des cahiers et des crayons. **4.** des tables de cuisine. **5.** des messages. **6.** des carottes. **7.** des bons anniversaires. **8.** des chaises bleues.

## REVIEW EXERCISE 3
**1.** There are (some) potatoes and (some) carrots on the table in the kitchen. **2.** Are you hungry? There is a croissant in the bag. **3.** At work, there are a lot of books on my desk. **4.** There are also (some) pens, (some) pencils and (some) notebooks. **5.** (Do) you prefer white flowers or a green plant? **6.** This is / It's a present for your birthday.

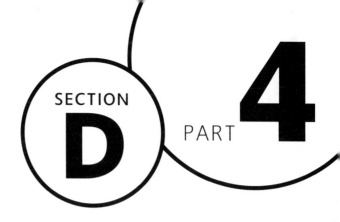

# *More Possessive Adjectives*

We've already covered a few possessive adjectives – *mon, ma, mes, ton, ta, tes,* and *son, sa, ses* to be exact. Now we're ready to add the plurals – "our," "their" and "your." But first, let's add some more vocabulary.

## POINT 1: VOCABULARY

| | |
|---|---|
| *toujours* | always |
| *souvent* | often |
| *jamais* | never |
| *rien de plus* | nothing else |
| *encore* | again / still |
| *vraiment* | really |
| *nouveau, nouvelle* | new (masc., fem.) |
| *ancien, -ne* | ancient, old |
| *vieux, vieille* | old (masc., fem.) |
| *jeune* | young |
| *sérieux, -se* | serious (masc., fem.) |
| *drôle* | funny |
| *intéressant, -e* | interesting (masc., fem.) |
| *bon, -ne* | good (masc., fem.) |

| | |
|---|---|
| *bien* | well |
| *parce que* | because |
| *pour* | for |
| *les chaussures* | the shoes |
| *les chaussons* | the slippers |

### PRACTICE EXERCISE 1

Fill in the blanks with one of the following words: *ancienne, parce que, drôle, pour, chaussons, jamais, nouveau, bons.*

1. *Je mange _____ j'ai faim.*
2. *Voici un cadeau _____ ton anniversaire.*
3. *La maison de mes grands-parents est très _____.*
4. *Pour la maison, j'ai des _____.*
5. *"_____" c'est le contraire (opposite) de "toujours."*
6. *"_____" c'est le contraire de "sérieux."*
7. *Vous avez un _____ message.*
8. *Les croissants sont très _____.*

> ## POINT 2: *LES ADJECTIFS POSSESSIFS*, THE REST OF THEM

You've already seen the first batch a lot throughout this course, but let's review anyway.

| | | | |
|---|---|---|---|
| **my** | mon | ma | mes |
| **your** | ton | ta | tes |
| **his /her/its** | son | sa | ses |

Remember that "my" will be *mon* or *ma* or *mes*, depending on the gender and number of what's being possessed: *mon frère (un frère), ma sœur (une sœur), mes parents (des parents).* The same is true of *ton/ta/tes* and *son/sa/ses.*

If this first group of possessive adjectives refers to one owner or possessor, then the new group refers to more than one owner or possessor.

| | | | |
|---|---|---|---|
| *our* | notre | notre | nos |
| *your (plural or polite)* | votre | votre | vos |
| *their* | leur | leur | leurs |

Did you notice that the singular forms are the same for masculine and feminine? It's *notre père* as well as *notre mère,* in other words. Unlike the singular, where you have to choose between *mon* or *ma* and *ton* or *ta,* you never have to worry about gender with *notre, votre,* and *leur.* You do, though, have to use the plural forms: *nos, vos,* and *leurs.*

And don't forget that *votre/vos* is not just the plural but also the polite form. You'd use it to mean "your" when talking to a group of friends, your siblings, your parents, etc., but also when you're talking to your professor, your boss, or a group of professors or bosses.

—*Alice et Charlotte, voici vos parents.*

—Alice and Charlotte, here are your parents.

—*Madame, c'est votre voiture.*

—Madam, this is your car.

—*Ce sont leurs frères et leurs femmes.*

—These are their brothers and their wives.

—*Bienvenue dans notre maison.*

—Welcome to our house.

—*Nos livres sont anciens.*

—Our books are old.

### PRACTICE EXERCISE 2

Fill in the blanks with the appropriate possessive adjectives. Use the words in parentheses as clues.

1. *J'habite dans _____ maison. (la maison de ma sœur)*
2. *Ce sont _____ chaussures ? (les chaussures de nos amis)*

3. *Ce n'est pas* _____ *voiture. (à nous)*

4. _____ *amis habitent à Reims. (mes amis et tes amis)*

5. _____ *enfants vont à l'université de Reims. (les enfants de ses amis)*

6. *C'est* _____ *appareil photo ? (à vous)*

7. *Voici* _____ *livres, Monsieur. (le professeur)*

8. _____ *chien est chez moi l (à toi)*

( **WATCH THE DVD** )

Are you ready for the DVD? Then watch Part 4, Section D before coming back for a review.

# *REVIEW EXERCISES*

### REVIEW EXERCISE 1

Translate each of the possessive adjectives in the following sentences.

1. (your, singular, familiar) *amis sont chez moi.*

2. *C'est* (your, singular, polite) *femme, Monsieur ?*

3. *Voici* (my) *chien l*

4. *Je vous présente* (my) *parents.*

5. (Our) *enfants sont à l'école avec* (their) *amie, Sonja.*

6. *Voilà* (my) *professeur de français et* (his) *femme.*

7. (Her) *sac est dans* (your, singular, familiar) *voiture.*

8. (Your, singular, familiar) *livres sont dans* (their) *bureaux.*

9. (Their) *maison n'est pas très grande, mais elle est très belle.*

10. *Est-ce que tu as* (my) *radio ?*

### REVIEW EXERCISE 2

Translate the following sentences.

1. *J' ai ton livre vert.*

2. *C'est son cadeau d'anniversaire ?*

3. *Quel âge a ton ami ?*
4. *Il a dix-sept ans et c'est son anniversaire.*
5. *Il est midi et nous avons faim et soif.*
6. *Voilà notre chien dans la cuisine.*
7. *Leur maison est très grande.*
8. *C'est la femme de votre ami.*
9. *Monsieur, vos voitures sont belles.*
10. *Mais je préfère ma bicyclette bleue.*

# *Answer Key*

**PRACTICE EXERCISE 1**

**1.** parce que  **2.** pour  **3.** ancienne  **4.** chaussons  **5.** jamais  **6.** drôle
**7.** nouveau  **8.** bons

**PRACTICE EXERCISE 2**

**1.** leur **2.** leurs **3.** notre **4.** Nos **5.** Leurs **6.** votre **7.** vos **8.** Ton

**REVIEW EXERCISE 1**

**1.** Tes **2.** votre **3.** mon **4.** mes **5.** Nos, leur **6.** mon, sa **7.** Son, ta **8.** Tes, leurs
**9.** Leur **10.** ma

**REVIEW EXERCISE 2**

**1.** I have your green book.  **2.** It's her/his birthday present?  **3.** How old is
your friend?  **4.** He's seventeen, and it's his birthday.  **5.** It's noon and we are
hungry and thirsty.  **6.** There's our dog in the kitchen.  **7.** Their house is very
big.  **8.** This is the wife of your friend.  **9.** Sir, your cars are beautiful.
**10.** But I prefer my blue bicycle.

# Mes Passe-Temps

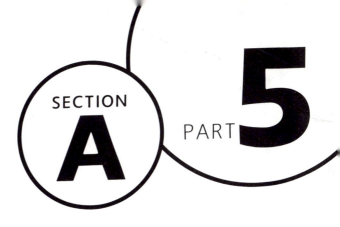

# SECTION A PART 5

## *Weather and the Calendar*

You can probably figure out that the name of Part 5, *Mes Passe-temps*, has something to do with, well, passing time. And how do plenty of people pass time? With hobbies, *bien sûr!* This compound may sound a bit odd, but at least it heralds a nice, fun part of the course. Which is good, since Part 5 is the last one, and in it you'll learn how to talk about what you do for fun, discuss the weather or the calendar, use some adverbs, ask questions, and finally, conjugate two very common and useful verbs, *aller* (to go) and *faire* (to do or to make.) But first, the vocabulary for Section A.

### POINT 1: VOCABULARY

This list may look a bit long, but that's just because we're covering days of the week and months of the year. As usual, take it slowly and repeat the words over and over again until they're familiar.

| | |
|---|---|
| *le jour* | the day |
| *la semaine* | the week |
| *la semaine dernière* | last week |
| *la semaine prochaine* | next week |
| *lundi* | Monday |
| *mardi* | Tuesday |

| | |
|---|---|
| mercredi | Wednesday |
| jeudi | Thursday |
| vendredi | Friday |
| samedi | Saturday |
| dimanche | Sunday |
| le week-end | the weekend |
| aujourd'hui | today |
| hier | yesterday |
| demain | tomorrow |
| le mois | the month |
| janvier | January |
| février | February |
| mars | March |
| avril | April |
| mai | May |
| juin | June |
| juillet | July |
| août | August |
| septembre | September |
| octobre | October |
| novembre | November |
| décembre | December |
| la date | the date |
| une / l'année | a / the year |
| la saison | the season |
| le printemps | spring |
| un / l'été | a / the summer |
| un / l'automne | a / the fall |
| un / l'hiver | a / the winter |
| le passe-temps | the hobby |
| passer | to spend |

| | |
|---|---|
| *le temps* | the time / the weather |
| *la météo(rologie)* | the meteo(rology) / the weather report |
| *la pluie* | the rain |
| *la neige* | the snow |
| *le vent* | the wind |
| *être en vacances* | to be on vacation |
| *faire du ski* | to ski |
| *un / l'arbre* | a / the tree |
| *être en fleurs* | to blossom |
| *une feuille* | a leaf |
| *la personne* | the person |
| *le premier, la première* | the first (masc. / fem.) |
| *en premier* | (at) first (adverb) |
| *la fête nationale* | the national holiday |
| *ce, cette* | this (masc. /fem.) |
| *chaque* | each |

## PRACTICE EXERCISE 1

Match the French word or expression in the left column with its English equivalent in the right column.

| | | |
|---|---|---|
| 1. | *faire du ski* | Wednesday |
| 2. | *parce que* | April |
| 3. | *commencer* | each |
| 4. | *mercredi* | at work |
| 5. | *avril* | because |
| 6. | *beaucoup de* | the first |
| 7. | *être en vacances* | a tree |
| 8. | *la semaine dernière* | the season |
| 9. | *au travail* | to start |
| 10. | *la saison* | a lot of |
| 11. | *chaque* | last week |

| 12. | *nager* | to be on vacation |
|-----|---------|-------------------|
| 13. | *le premier* | to ski |
| 14. | *un arbre* | to swim |

### PRACTICE EXERCISE 2

Fill in the blanks with the most logical word or expression.

1. *L'hiver, l'automne, le printemps, et l'été sont des _____.*

2. *Mardi est avant _____.*

3. *Jeudi est avant _____.*

4. *Il y a douze _____ dans l'année.*

5. *Mon frère est sportif. Il aime _____ du sport.*

6. *En été, il n'y a pas d'école : les enfants sont _____*

7. *Après l'hiver, c'est le _____.*

8. *En hiver, mes amis aiment faire du _____.*

9. *Le week-end commence _____.*

10. *Le p_____ jour de travail, c'est lundi.*

---

## POINT 2: *QUEL TEMPS FAIT-IL ?* / WHAT IS THE WEATHER?

To ask about the weather, just use the question *Quel temps fait-il ?* After all, it can be very useful to be able to talk about the weather, you know, just to be able to fill in any embarrassing pauses in casual conversations.

| | |
|---|---|
| Alice: | *Bonjour, comment ça va ?* |
| Charlotte: | *Ça va bien, merci et toi ?* |
| Alice: | *Comme ci comme ça . . . Ah, quel mauvais temps !* |
| Charlotte: | *Oui, il pleut toujours.* |
| Alice: | *Oui . . . Moi, je vais au ciné. Alors, salut !* |
| Charlotte: | *Au revoir . . .* |

If Charlotte and Alice hadn't spoken to each other about the weather, well, they really wouldn't have said much at all. Just in case you didn't catch every word, here it is again in English.

Alice:          Hello, how are you?
Charlotte:      I'm fine, thanks, and you?
Alice:          Okay. Ah, what awful weather!
Charlotee:      Yeah, it rains all the time!
Alice:          Yes . . . I'm going to the movies. So, good-bye!
Charlotte:      Bye . . .

And here are some great weather-related expressions that you can use to jump start a conversation, or at least fill in the gaps! Notice that a lot of them use the verb *faire*, "to do" or "to make." You'll study that verb more later on.

—*Quel temps fait-il ?*
—What's the weather like?
—*Il fait mauvais.*
—The weather is bad.
—*Il fait beau.*
—The weather is beautiful.
—*Il fait (du) soleil.*
—It's sunny.
—*Il fait chaud.*
—It's hot.
—*Il fait gris.*
—The sky is gray.
—*Il fait nuageux.*
—It's cloudy.
—*Il fait froid.*
—It's cold.
—*Il fait frais.*
—It's chilly.

—*Il fait du vent.*
—It's windy.
—*Quel mauvais temps !*
—What bad weather!
—*Quel beau temps !*
—What beautiful weather!

There are two verbs that you use on their own, without *faire*: *pleuvoir* and *neiger*, "to rain" and "to snow." Of course, you have to conjugate them, but you only use them with *il*:
—*Il pleut.*
—It's raining.
—*Il neige.*
—It's snowing.

### PRACTICE EXERCISE 3

Classify each of the following weather expressions under the heading *il fait beau* or *il fait mauvais*. Then, translate each one:

*il fait soleil, il pleut, il fait froid, il fait gris, il neige, il fait nuageux, il fait chaud, il fait frais.*

1. *Il fait beau :*
2. *Il fait mauvais :*

### POINT 3: *LES QUATRE SAISONS*

Yes, we're talking about the four seasons. So, *les quatre saisons . . . Quelles sont-elles ?* (What are they?)
—*Les quatre saisons sont : le printemps, l'été, l'automne, l'hiver.*
—The four seasons are: spring, summer, fall, winter.

*—Au printemps, il fait frais et il pleut.*
—In spring, it's chilly and it rains.
*—En été, il y a du soleil et il fait chaud.*
—In summer, it's sunny and hot.
*—En automne, il fait froid et il y a du vent.*
—In fall, it's cold and windy.
*—En hiver, il fait froid et il neige.*
—In winter, it's cold and snowing.

As you see, to say "in" a particular season, each season name is preceded by the little word *en.*
*—en été, en automne, en hiver . . .*
—in summer, in fall, winter . . .

But of course there's an exception!
*—au printemps*
—in spring

**PRACTICE EXERCISE 4**

Replace the English words in the following sentences with their equivalents in French.

1. *Le* (spring) *est ma saison préférée.*
2. (In winter), *nous aimons faire du ski.*
3. *Les feuilles des arbres sont rouges et marron* (in fall).
4. *On est à la plage tous les* (summers).
5. *Tous les arbres sont en fleurs* (in spring).
6. *En* (summer) *il fait très chaud !*
7. *Il fait froid et il fait du vent* (in winter).
8. *Il ne* (snows) *pas en été.*
9. *La première saison de l'année est l'* (winter).
10. *L'école commence en* (fall).

## POINT 4: *LES JOURS DE LA SEMAINE*

Now let's go back over the days of the week. *Les jours de la semaine en français sont :*

*lundi* / Monday

*mardi* / Tuesday

*mercredi* / Wednesday

*jeudi* / Thursday

*vendredi* / Friday

*samedi* / Saturday

*dimanche* / Sunday

*Deux ou trois petites choses.* (Two or three things.) Notice *en premier* (first) that in French, the days of the week are not capitalized. *Et puis* (and then), in France, the week doesn't start on Sunday, but *le lundi*. Finally, all the days of the week are masculine.

Days are used without articles when you're talking about a specific, upcoming day. This is the equivalent of the English "on Monday" or "on Friday."

—*Lundi, l'école commence.*

—School starts on Monday.

—*Fabienne va au Québec mercredi.*

—Fabienne is going to Quebec on Wednesday.

But to talk about something that happens regularly, the equivalent of the English "Monday<u>s</u>" or "Friday<u>s</u>," the article *le* is used:

—*Le jeudi, je vais au travail. (= tous les jeudis)*

—Thursdays, I go to work. (= every Thursday)

—*Nous avons toujours sommeil le lundi.*

—We're always sleepy Mondays.

Here are some other examples to practice with:

—*La semaine a sept jours.*

—The week has seven days.

—*Le premier jour de la semaine est lundi.*

—The first day of the week is Monday.

—*Lundi est aussi le premier jour de travail.*

—Monday is also the first day of work.

—*Mercredi est avant jeudi.*

—Wednesday is before Thursday.

—*Samedi est après vendredi.*

—Saturday is after Friday.

—*Aujourd'hui, c'est lundi et demain, c'est mardi.*

—Today, it's Monday and tomorrow, it's Tuesday.

—*Le week-end, c'est samedi et dimanche.*

—The weekend is Saturday and Sunday.

**PRACTICE EXERCISE 5**

Choose your favorite chores or activities for each day of the week by connecting the days on the left to a phrase on the right. Then repeat each sentence out loud.

1. *Le lundi,*         *je fais le ménage.*
2. *Le mardi,*         *je vais au musée.*
3. *Le mercredi,*      *je vais à la plage.*
4. *Le jeudi,*         *je suis au travail.*
5. *Le vendredi,*      *je fais la lessive.* (laundry)
6. *Le samedi,*        *je vais au supermarché.*
7. *Le dimanche,*      *je regarde la télévision.*
8. *Le week-end,*      *je suis à la maison.*

Let's keep on exploring *le calendrier* by looking at the months of the year, or *les mois de l'année*.

*janvier* / January

*février* / February

*mars* / March

*avril* / April

*mai* / May

*juin* / June

*juillet* / July

*août* / August

*septembre* / September

*octobre* / October

*novembre* / November

*décembre* / December

Aren't you lucky that *les mois* are pretty similar to the months? And, as you can guess, it's not just to make it easier for you, but because of their common roots in Latin. Also, have you noticed that the names of the months, like the days, are not capitalized either? Here are a few sentences to practice all that you've seen so far.

—*Janvier est le premier mois de l'année et il fait très froid parce que c'est l'hiver.*

—January is the first month of the year, and it's very cold, because it's winter.

—*En hiver, j'aime faire du ski quand il neige.*

—In winter, I like to ski when it snows.

—*Et parce qu'il fait froid, je vais aussi au cinéma et au musée.*

—And because it's cold, I also go to the movies and to the museum.

—*En été, quand il fait chaud, je préfère aller à la piscine.*

—In summer, when it's hot, I prefer to go to the swimming pool.

—*J'adore nager toute l'année.*

—I love to swim all year long.

—*Et puis, je fais du sport tous les jours de la semaine.*

—And then, I play sports every day of the week.

—*Le week-end, j'aime aller au stade et regarder les matchs de foot.*

—On the weekend, I like to go to the stadium and watch the soccer games.

## POINT 6: *QUELLE EST LA DATE D'AUJOURD'HUI ?*

What's today's date? Well, to answer this question, you have to know all the necessary ingredients, which luckily you do.

—*Le nom des jours :*
*lundi, mardi, mercredi, jeudi, vendredi, samedi, dimanche.*

—*Le nom des mois :*
*janvier, février, mars, avril, mai, juin, juillet, août, septembre, octobre, novembre, décembre.*

—*Et . . .* you can count up to 21: *un, deux, trois, quatre, cinq, six, sept, huit, neuf, dix, onze, douze, treize, quatorze, quinze, seize, dix-sept, dix-huit, dix-neuf, vingt, vingt et un.* But, since there are a few more days in a month, and they're not so hard to learn, here are the rest of the numbers up to 31: *vingt-deux, vingt-trois, vingt-quatre, vingt-cinq, vingt-six, vingt-sept, vingt-huit, vingt-neuf, trente et un.*

To write *la date en français*, you put the day first, then the date, then the month. That's it! And remember, no capital letter for the days and months. For instance:

—*La date d'aujourd'hui est samedi 14 février.*

—Today's date is Saturday, February 14.

—*Aujourd'hui, c'est lundi 16 juin.*

—Today, it's Monday, June 16.

—*Demain, c'est dimanche 5 janvier*

—Tomorrow, it's Sunday, January 5.

But to say "on" a particular date, you need to use *le*:

—*Elle commence le travail le 7 décembre.*

—She starts work on December 7.

### PRACTICE EXERCISE 6

*Pour chaque saison, il y a quatre mois.* Write all the months for each season:

1. *L'hiver :*

2. *Le printemps :*

3. *L'été :*

4. *L'automne :*

( **WATCH THE DVD** )

Now go and check out Part 5, Section A, on your DVD.

# *REVIEW EXERCISES*

### REVIEW EXERCISE 1

Translate each of the following sentences into English.

1. *On aime l'été, parce qu'on est en vacances.*

2. *Mes mois favoris sont juillet et août parce que je vais nager tous les jours.*

3. *Je vais à l' université le lundi, le mardi et le jeudi.*

4. *Cette semaine, je commence un nouveau travail.*

5. *Vendredi 28 mars, je vais au musée avec mes parents.*

6. *Au printemps, il pleut chaque jour.*

7. *Quel est le temps ce week-end ?*

8. *Quelle est la date d'aujourd'hu i? Et de demain ?*

9. *La semaine commence le lundi en France.*

10. *Le temps est beau au printemps, en été et en automne. Mais il fait frais en hiver.*

### REVIEW EXERCISE 2

Answer each of the following.

1. Friday, February 14, 2005, is *en français:* _____.

2. Saturday, June 7 is: _____.

3. *Quels sont les mois du printemps ?*

4. *Ce week-end, il fait* (beautiful and sunny.)

5. *Une semaine a* _____ *jours.*

6. *En* _____ *les feuilles sont rouges, jaunes, et oranges.*

7. *En France, la semaine commence le lundi ou le dimanche ?*

8. *Il y a* _____ *saisons.*

### REVIEW EXERCISE 3

For each of the following events, write the appropriate date.

1. *La date du premier jour de l'année est :* _____.

2. *Mon anniversaire est le :* _____.

3. *La fête nationale de États-Unis est :* _____.

4. *Le premier jour du printemps est :* _____.

5. *La fête de* Martin Luther King, Jr. *est :* _____. ("Third" is *troisième*.")

6. Labor day *est :* _____.

7. Thanksgiving *aux États-Unis est :* _____. ("Last" is *dernier*.)

8. Veteran's Day *est :* _____.

# *Answer Key*

**PRACTICE EXERCISE 1**

**1.** faire du ski – to ski  **2.** parce que – because  **3.** commencer – to start
**4.** mercredi – Wednesday  **5.** avril – April  **6.** beaucoup de – a lot of  **7.** être en
vacances – to be on vacation  **8.** la semaine dernière – last week  **9.** au travail
– at work  **10.** la saison – the season  **11.** chaque – each  **12.** nager – to swim
**13.** le premier – the first  **14.** un arbre – a tree

**PRACTICE EXERCISE 2**

**1.** saisons  **2.** mercredi.  **3.** vendredi  **4.** mois  **5.** faire  **6.** en vacances
**7.** printemps  **8.** ski  **9.** samedi  **10.** premier

**PRACTICE EXERCISE 3**

**1.** Il fait beau : il fait soleil (it's sunny), il fait chaud (it's hot), il fait frais (it's
chilly).  **2.** Il fait mauvais : il pleut (it's raining), il fait froid (it's cold), il fait gris
(the sky is gray), il neige (it's snowing), il fait nuageux (it's cloudy).

**PRACTICE EXERCISE 4**

**1.** printemps  **2.** En hiver  **3.** en automne  **4.** étés  **5.** au printemps  **6.** été  **7.** en
hiver  **8.** neige  **9.** hiver  **10.** automne

**PRACTICE EXERCISE 5**

(The combinations are up to you.)

**PRACTICE EXERCISE 6**

**1.** L'hiver : décembre, janvier, février, mars.  **2.** Le printemps : mars, avril, mai,
juin.  **3.** L'été : juin, juillet, août, septembre.  **4.** L'automne : septembre,
octobre, novembre, décembre.

**REVIEW EXERCISE 1**

**1.** We like summer because we are on vacation.   **2.** My favorite months are July and August because I go swimming every day.   **3.** I go to the university Mondays, Tuesdays, and Thursdays.   **4.** This week, I start a new job.   **5.** Friday, March 28, I go to the museum with my parents.   **6.** In spring, it rains every day.   **7.** What is the weather (like) for this weekend?   **8.** What is the date today? And tomorrow?   **9.** The week starts on Monday in France.   **10.** The weather is beautiful in spring, summer and fall. But it's chilly in winter.

**REVIEW EXERCISE 2**

**1.** vendredi 14 février 2005   **2.** samedi 7 juin   **3.** mars, avril, mai, juin.   **4.** beau et il fait du soleil.   **5.** sept .   **6.** automne   **7.**  le lundi   **8.** quatre.

**REVIEW EXERCISE 3**

**1.** Le premier janvier   **2.** For example: le 27 janvier.   **3.** Le 4 juillet   **4.** Le 21 mars   **5.** Le troisième lundi de janvier   **6.** Le premier lundi de septembre   **7.** Le dernier jeudi de novembre   **8.** Le 11 novembre

## The Verbs ALLER and FAIRE

**POINT 1:** VOCABULARY

| | |
|---|---|
| *aller* | to go |
| *aller au travail* | to go to work |
| *les vacances* | holidays |
| *aller en vacances* | to go on vacation |
| *la piscine* | the swimming pool |
| *la plage* | the beach |
| *le stade* | the stadium |
| *le ski* | the ski |
| *faire* | to do / make |
| *faire du ski* | to ski |
| *la cuisine* | the cooking / the kitchen |
| *faire la cuisine* | to cook |
| *le ménage* | the house cleaning |
| *faire le ménage* | to do the house cleaning |
| *la vaisselle* | the dishes |
| *faire la vaisselle* | to do the dishes |
| *essuyer la vaisselle* | to dry the dishes |
| *faire les devoirs* | to do homework |

| | |
|---|---|
| *la promenade* | the walk |
| *faire une promenade* | to go for a walk |
| *la balade en voiture* | the car ride (colloquial) |
| *le voyage* | the trip |
| *faire un voyage* | to go on a trip |
| *voyager* | to travel |
| *Fais bon voyage!* | Have a nice trip! |
| *le musée* | the museum |
| *tous les jours /* | each day / every day |
| *chaque jour* | |
| *les gens* | people |

## PRACTICE EXERCISE 1

Fill in the blanks with the appropriate vocabulary word.

1.  *En été, je vais tous les jours à la _____.*
2.  *En hiver, j'aime _____ du ski.*
3.  *Un bon étudiant aime faire ses _____.*
4.  *Tu vas en France ? Fais bon _____ !*
5.  *À la maison, je n'aime pas faire le _____.*
6.  *Mais je préfère _____ la vaisselle.*
7.  *Mon ami adore faire la _____ pour moi, parce que j'ai toujours faim !*
8.  *L'été, les gens vont en _____.*

**POINT 2:** THE CONJUGATION AND USE OF *ALLER*

*Aller* is yet another irregular verb, but this shouldn't make you scream and run away, because it's pretty easy. Actually, you've already been using it throughout the course. *Comment* <u>*vas*</u>-*tu ?, je* <u>*vais*</u> *bien, ça* <u>*va*</u> … But naturally, you still have to memorize the rest of the conjugation. *Allez* ! (Let's go!)

| | |
|---|---|
| *je vais* | I go, I am going, I do go |
| *tu vas* | you go, you are going, you do go |

| | |
|---|---|
| *il / elle / on va* | he / she / it / one goes, etc. |
| *nous allons* | we go |
| *vous allez* | you go |
| *ils / elles vont* | they go |

Don't forget the liaison in *nous allons* [noo-zah-loh*n] and *vous allez* [voo-zah-lay.] And just as the English "to go" is usually followed by the preposition "to," in French, *aller* is usually followed by *à* ("to"), *au / aux* ("to the") or *en* ("in" / "on").

—*Je vais en vacances le mois prochain.*

—I'm going on vacation next month.

—*Tu vas au ski ?*

—You're going to ski?

—*Nous allons à la piscine ce week-end.*

—We're going to the swimming pool this weekend.

—*Ils ne vont pas à l'université cette année.*

—They don't go to the university this year.

—*J'adore aller à la plage.*

—I love to go to the beach.

—*Mais je vais aussi au cinéma.*

—But I also go to the movies.

—*Carlos et moi allons souvent au stade.*

—Carlos and I often go to the stadium.

—*Et quand il est avec sa famille, il va au musée.*

—And when he is with his family, he goes to the museum.

—*Pour leurs vacances, ils vont aux États-Unis.*

—For their vacation, they're going to the States.

**PRACTICE EXERCISE 2**

In each of the following sentences, replace the infinitive with the correct conjugated form of *aller*.

1. *Nous (aller) au cinéma samedi.*
2. *Je (aller) à la piscine quand il fait beau.*
3. *Pourquoi (aller)-tu au ski ?*
4. *Vous (aller) à l'université ?*
5. *Elles (aller) au marché tous les lundis.*
6. *Le mois prochain, il (aller) en France.*
7. *Je ne (aller) pas au musée demain.*
8. *Elle ne (aller) pas au stade.*
9. *Mes amis et moi (aller) au travail.*
10. *Tu (aller) à la plage avec ce mauvais temps ?*

> **POINT 3:** THE CONJUGATION OF *FAIRE*

And here's the second very important and common irregular verb you'll meet in Section B of Part 5. *Faire* means "to do" or "to make," and it's used a lot. But first, its conjugation. Again, look for some patterns you might notice among the conjugations of *être*, *avoir*, *aller*, and *faire*.

*je fais* – I do/I make, I am doing/I am making, I do do/I do make
*tu fais* – you do/make, etc.
*il / elle / on fait* – he / she / it / one does/makes, etc.
*nous faisons* [noofuhzon] – we do (make)
*vous faites* – you do (make)
*ils / elles font* – they do (make)

Just a quick note on pronunciation. In the singular, the *ai* is pronounced like "eh", so *fais*, *fais*, and *fait* all sound like [feh.] But in the *nous* form, the *ai* sounds like "uh," so *faisons* is [fuh-zoh*n.] In the *vous* form, the *ai* is back to "eh", so *faites* sounds like [feht.]

*Faire* is quite easy, and it's a very useful verb tool There are many expressions or idioms with *faire*. Some have nice, literal translations in English, but a lot do not.

—*Qu'est-ce que tu fais ?*

—What do you do? / What are you doing?

—*Je fais les devoirs.*

—I'm doing homework.

—*Il fait chaud.*

—It's hot.

—*Marc fait son lit.*

—Marc is making his bed.

—*Mon ami fait la cuisine tous les soirs.*

—My friend cooks every evening.

—*Ils font du ski en hiver.*

—They ski in winter.

—*Mon amie fait la lessive chaque dimanche.*

—My friend does the laundry every Sunday.

—*Tu ne fais jamais le ménage !*

—You never clean up the house! / You never do the house cleaning!

—*Elles font une promenade en voiture.*

—They're driving around. / They're taking a drive.

—*Nous faisons beaucoup de sport.*

—We do a lot of sports.

—*Vous faites une balade ?*

—You're taking a walk? / You're going for a walk?

—*Elle fait la vaisselle le midi, et moi, le soir.*

—She does the dishes at noon, and I do them in the evening.

—*Fais bon voyage ! / Faites bon voyage !*

—Have a nice trip!

And of course, you remember how to describe the weather with *il fait chaud,
il fait froid, il fait gris, il fait beau, il fait mauvais, il fait du soleil* . . .

### PRACTICE EXERCISE 3
Find the second part for each sentence and read the sentence aloud.

1.  *Elle ne*                *faisons pas la cuisine.*
2.  *Elles*                  *fais rien.*
3.  *Nous ne*                *fait les devoirs.*
4.  *Vous*                   *fais souvent du sport.*
5.  *Tu*                     *fait beau.*
6.  *Je ne*                  *font du ski.*
7.  *Il*                     *ne font pas de promenade en voiture aujourd'hui.*
8.  *Les parents ne*         *fais ?*
9.  *Mon petit frère*        *fait jamais la vaisselle.*
10. *Qu'est-ce que tu*       *faites le ménage tous les jours.*

( **WATCH THE DVD** )

If you've digested *aller* and *faire*, then it's time to watch Part 5, Section B on
your DVD.

## *REVIEW EXERCISES*

### REVIEW EXERCISE 1
Is it *faire* or *aller*? Choose the appropriate verb and its correct form.

1.  *Mes amis et moi (?) du ski chaque hiver.*
2.  *Tu (?) la vaisselle après le dîner ?*
3.  *Vous (?) au travail du lundi au vendredi.*
4.  *Nous (?) en voyage samedi prochain.*

5. *Mes sœurs n'aiment pas (?) le ménage.*
6. *Elles (?) à Marseille tous les week-ends.*
7. *Vous (?) la cuisine ce soir ?*
8. *Ils (?) beaucoup de sports.*
9. *Tu veux (?) une balade en voiture ?*
10. *Les enfants ne (?) pas leurs devoirs.*

### REVIEW EXERCISE 2

Rewrite the following sentences putting the words in the right order.

1. *balade / dimanche / une / fait / On / en / voiture.*
2. *déteste / la / vaisselle/ faire / Je.*
3. *la / bien / fait / Il / cuisine.*
4. *beaucoup / devoirs / Les / de / ont / étudiants.*
5. *jamais / le / ménage / ne / Elle / fait.*
6. *sport / bon / est / Nager / un.*

### REVIEW EXERCISE 3

Fill in each of the blanks in the following dialog with one of these words:
*stade, va, soir, neuf, merci, match, plage, piscine, allons, sport, ballade, allons*

| Serge: | *Salut, Christine ! Comment ça - _____ ?* |
| Christine: | *Ça va bien, _____ Quoi de _____ ?* |
| Serge: | *Et bien, Hervé et moi, nous _____ à la _____.* |
| Christine: | *Ah oui ? Il fait très chaud. Mais, nous, on va au _____.* |
| Serge: | *Vous faites du _____ aujourd'hui ?* |
| Christine: | *Non, il y a un _____ de foot.* |
| Serge: | *Ce _____ on va faire une _____ en voiture à la plage.* |
| Christine: | *Bien, c'est super ! Nous _____ aussi à la _____.* |

# Answer Key

**PRACTICE EXERCISE 1:**

**1.** plage / piscine **2.** faire **3.** devoirs **4.** voyage **5.** ménage **6.** faire **7.** cuisine
**8.** vacances

**PRACTICE EXERCISE 2**

**1.** allons **2.** vais **3.** vas **4.** allez **5.** vont **6.** va **7.** vais **8.** va **9.** allons **10.** vas

**PRACTICE EXERCISE 3**

**1.** Elle ne fait jamais la vaisselle. **2.** Elles font du ski. **3.** Nous ne faisons pas
la cuisine. **4.** Vous faites le ménage tous les jours. **5.** Tu fais souvent du
sport. **6.** Je ne fais rien. **7.** Il fait beau. **8.** Les parents ne font pas
de promenade en voiture aujourd'hui. **9.** Mon petit frère fait les devoirs.
**10.** Qu'est-ce que tu fais ?

**REVIEW EXERCISE 1**

**1.** faisons **2.** fais **3.** allez **4.** allons **5.** faire **6.** vont **7.** faites **8.** font **9.** faire
**10.** font

**REVIEW EXERCISE 2**

**1.** On fait une balade en voiture dimanche. **2.** Je déteste faire la vaisselle.
**3.** Il fait bien la cuisine. **4.** Les étudiants ont beaucoup de devoirs. **5.** Elle ne
fait jamais le ménage. **6.** Nager est un bon sport.

**REVIEW EXERCISE 3**

**1.** va **2.** merci / neuf **3.** allons/piscine **4.** stade **5.** sport **6.** match **7.** soir /
balade **8.** allons / plage

SECTION C

PART 5

## *Questions*

You've been seeing questions all throughout this course, and now we're going to take a closer look at how to form them. But as usual, we'll start with some vocabulary.

> **POINT 1:** VOCABULARY

| | |
|---|---|
| *la pomme* | the apple |
| *commencer* | to start, to begin |
| *donner* | to give |
| *en* | in / by |
| *à* | to, at |
| *quand* | when |
| *que* | what |
| *qui* | who |
| *où* | where |
| *comment* | how |
| *pourquoi* | why |
| *quel(-s), quelle(-s)* | what / which |
| *parce que* | because |

**PRACTICE EXERCISE 1**

Fill in the blanks in these questions and answers with the appropriate words.

1. *Tu* (go) *en vacances ?*
2. *Je vais* (on) *vacances cet été.*
3. (Where) *allez vous?*
4. *Nous allons* (to) *la plage.*
5. *Ils vont au* (stadium) *?*
6. (Today) *il y a un match de foot.*
7. *Quelle est la* (date) *d'aujourd'hui ?*
8. *Aujourd'hui il fait* (very hot).

## POINT 2: FORMING QUESTIONS

You've already learned how to express a question just by raising the intonation. The order of words in your question stays exactly the same, just as in English.

—*Tu aimes le rap ?*

—You like rap?

—*Tu as des frères et des sœurs ?*

—You have brothers and sisters?

But just like in English, there are other ways to ask a question in French. In English, you normally form a question by inverting the word order ("is he?" instead of "he is . . . ") or by adding an helping verb ("does she go?" instead of "she goes . . . ") In French, you normally just invert the word order, putting the verb first in the sentence. There's never any helping verb that you have to insert. So . . .

—*Tu as un chat.* (You have a cat.)

becomes:

—*As-tu un chat ?* (Do you have a cat?)

*—Elles vont à la piscine.* (They're going to the pool.)
becomes:
*—Vont-elles à la piscine ?* (Are they going to the pool?)

*—Il est au bureau.* (He is at the office.)
becomes:
*—Est-il au bureau ?* (Is he at at the office?)

It's actually pretty simple. Invert the order of subject and verb so that the verb comes first. If the subject of the sentence is a pronoun (such as *tu* or *elles* or *il* in the examples above) you get to insert a cool hyphen between verb and subject.

Two little things to keep in mind. First, if the verb ends in a vowel and the subject pronoun starts with a vowel (*il, elle, on*) too, you've got to add a *-t-*, the letter *t* framed by two hyphens, right after the verb but before the pronoun. That way, it sounds nicer.
*—On a des devoirs.* (We've got some homework.)
*—A-t-on des devoirs ?* (Do we have any homework?)
*—Elle aime le théâtre.* (She likes the theater.)
*—Aime-t-elle le théâtre ?* (Does she like the theater?)
*—Elle va à l'université.* (She's going to the university.)
*—Va-t-elle à l'université ?* (Is she going to the university?)

The second little thing to keep in mind is that you usually can't use inversion to form a question with *je*. In other words, you can say: *Je chante bien.* But you cannot say: *Chante-je bien ?* Does that mean that there are no questions with "I" in French? Of course not. Luckily, there's a third and very common way to form a question, and that's simply to start with the phrase: *Est-ce que . . . ?*

*Est-ce que* . . . means something like "Is it that . . . " or "Is it the case that . . . "
But it doesn't sound weird and stilted in French! It just means that whatever
follows it is a question, even though the word order is the same. And don't
forget that *que* will become *qu'* in front of vowel sounds – the famous elision.

—*Est-ce que je chante bien* ?

—Do I sing well?

—*Est-ce que ton professeur est sympathique* ?

—Is your professor friendly?

—*Est-ce qu'ils vont au stade ce weekend* ?

—Are they going to the stadium this weekend?

—*Est-ce que vous parlez français* ?

—Do you speak French?


### PRACTICE EXERCISE 2

Please rewrite these statements as questions using inversion.

1. *Nous avons des pommes.*
2. *Ils sont très gentils.*
3. *Elle aime aller à la piscine.*
4. *Vous allez à la plage.*
5. *Ils font la lessive.*


### PRACTICE EXERCISE 3

Now rewrite the same statements as questions using *Est-ce que* . . .


## POINT 3: QUESTIONS WITH INTERROGATIVES

Not all questions have yes/no answers. Some questions ask for other
information, and that's why we have interrogatives, which are in English
who, what, where, when, how, and why.

| | |
|---|---|
| *que* | what |
| *qui* | who |

| *quand* | when |
| *où* | where |
| *comment* | how |
| *pourquoi* | why |

These words are put at the beginning of the sentence, and then it's the same old story for inversion. So, it's INTERROGATIVE + VERB + SUBJECT + REST OF SENTENCE.

—*Que fait-il ?*

—What does he do? / What is he doing?

—*Où vas-tu ce soir ?*

—Where are you going tonight?

—*Qui est ton professeur ?*

—Who's your teacher?

—*Quand allez-vous au stade ?*

—When do you go to the stadium?

—*Où est ta nouvelle voiture ?*

—Where is your new car?

—*Pourquoi faites-vous du sport ?*

—Why do you do sports?

If the question starts with *pourquoi*, you answer with *parce que* (because):

—*Je fais du sport parce que j'aime ça.*

—I play sports because I like that.

—*Je vais au stade parce qu'il y a un match de foot.*

—I'm going to the stadium because there's a soccer game.

In the last sentence, *parce que* has changed to *parce qu'* because the following word, *il*, starts with a vowel. Yes, you're right, it's another case of elision, just to make the sentence run more smoothly.

**PRACTICE EXERCISE 4**

Rewrite the following questions putting the words in the right order.

1. *tes / Fais / -tu / devoirs ?*
2. *Pourquoi / à / Boston / allez / -vous ?*
3. *ami / habite / ton / Où ?*
4. *-t- / mange / Que / il ?*
5. *faites /du / -vous / Où / ski ?*

---

**POINT 4:** THE PREPOSITION À

By now, you're familiar with this little word, which can come after certain verbs like *aller, habiter, donner,* or *être* to express destination, location or intention:

—*Je donne le cadeau à mon ami.*

—I'm giving the gift to my friend.

—*Nous allons à la plage.*

—We're going to the beach.

—*J'habite à Nîmes.*

—I live in Nîmes.

—*Ils sont à la piscine.*

—They are at the swimming pool.

When *à* is followed by a definite article (*le, la,* or *les*) it has two special forms. *À* + *la* remains *à la* and *à* + *l'* remains *à l'*, but *à* + *le* becomes *au,* and *à* + *les* becomes *aux.*

—*Les enfants sont à la bibliothèque.*

—The children are at the library.

—*Mon frère va à l'école.*

—My brother is going to the school.

—*Monsieur Dufort est au stade.*

—Mr. Dufort is at the stadium.

—*Mes amis habitent aux États-Unis.*
—My friends live in the United States.

**PRACTICE EXERCISE 5**

Complete the following sentences accordingly with *à, au, à la, aux* or *à l'*:

1. *Mes amis vont _____ Canada pour le weekend.*
2. *Vas-tu _____ université ?*
3. *Elle va _____ travail tous les jours.*
4. *Vous habitez _____ Bordeaux ?*
5. *En décembre, elles font un voyage _____ États-Unis.*
6. *Nos parents sont _____ ski.*
7. *Dimanche, je vais _____ stade.*
8. *Il va _____ maison.*
9. *Nous allons _____ cinéma vendredi soir.*
10. *Ils font une promenade _____ musées de la ville.*
11. *Elle aime aller _____ parcs à Paris.*
12. *Donnes-tu la pomme _____ professeur de français ?*

( **WATCH THE DVD** )

Allez I Watch Part 5, Section C, on your DVDI

# *REVIEW EXERCISES*

**REVIEW EXERCISE 1**

Translate the following sentences.

1. When are they going on vacations?
2. Are you (sing. / familiar) at the stadium with your friends?
3. Why does she travel to the US?

4. I go to the swimming pool Wednesdays.
5. How is she doing?

### REVIEW EXERCISE 2

Complete each sentence with the correct form of the verb.

1. (go) -*tu au marché ce matin ?*
2. *Non, parce que je* (do) *du sport.*
3. *Nous* (go) *en vacances au mois de juillet.*
4. *Où* (go) -*vous en vacances ?*
5. *Ils* (do) *du sport tous les jours au stade.*
6. *Vous* (like) *nager ?*
7. *J'* (adore) (to swim) *à la piscine quand il n' y* (have) *personne.*
8. *Tu ne* (prefer) *pas la plage ?*

### REVIEW EXERCISE 3

Rewrite each of the following statements as questions. Use both inversion and *est-ce que* whenever possible, or an interrogative if one is given.

1. *Tous les hivers, elles font du ski. (Quand ?)*
2. *Ils vont à Venise.*
3. *Il fait froid ce matin.*
4. *Son anniversaire est le premier janvier. (Quand ?)*
5. *Elles vont au marché. (Où ?)*
6. *Ils vont au stade parce qu'il y a un match. (Pourquoi ?)*

# Answer Key

### PRACTICE EXERCISE 1

**1.** vas **2.** en **3.** Où **4.** à **5.** stade **6.** Aujourd'hui **7.** date **8.** très chaud

### PRACTICE EXERCISE 2

**1.** Avons-nous des pommes ? **2.** Sont-ils très gentils ? **3.** Aime-t-elle aller à la piscine ? **4.** Allez-vous à la plage ? **5.** Font-ils la lessive ?

### PRACTICE EXERCISE 3

**1.** Est-ce que nous avons des pommes ?   **2.** Est-ce qu'ils sont très gentils ?
**3.** Est-ce qu'elle aime aller à la piscine ?   **4.** Est-ce que vous allez à la plage ?
**5.** Est-ce qu'ils font la lessive ?

### PRACTICE EXERCISE 4

**1.** Fais-tu tes devoirs ?   **2.** Pourquoi allez-vous à Boston ?   **3.** Où habite ton
ami ?   **4.** Que mange-t-il ?   **5.** Où faites-vous du ski ?

### PRACTICE EXERCISE 5

**1.** au  **2.** à l'  **3.** au  **4.** à  **5.** aux  **6.** au  **7.** au  **8.** à la  **9.** au  **10.** aux  **11.** aux  **12.** au

### REVIEW EXERCISE 1

**1.** Quand vont-ils en vacances ?   **2.** Es-tu au stade avec tes amis ?
**3.** Pourquoi voyage-t-elle aux États-Unis ?   **4.** Je vais à la piscine le mercredi.
**5.** Comment va-t-elle  ?

### REVIEW EXERCISE 2

**1.** Vas  **2.** fais  **3.** allons  **4.** allez  **5.** font  **6.** aimez  **7.** adore / nager / a  **8.** préfères

### REVIEW EXERCISE 3

**1.** Quand font-elles du ski ?  **2.** Vont-ils à Venise ? / Est-ce qu'ils vont à Venise ?
**3.** Fait-il froid ce matin ? / Est-ce qu'il fait froid ce matin ?  **4.** Quand est son
anniversaire ?  **5.** Où vont-elles ?  **6.** Pourquoi vont-ils au stade ?

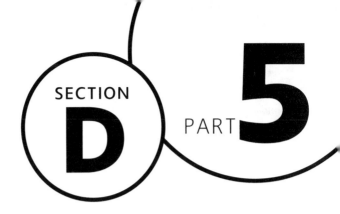

# Adverbs

In French as in English, adverbs do things like describe how or when some action is carried out (successfully, often, never) or how something is done (well, poorly, quickly.) They can also give more details about an adjective (<u>very</u> beautiful, <u>extremely</u> beautiful, <u>unbelievably</u> beautiful). But before we get to that, let's learn some new words.

**POINT 1:** VOCABULARY

| | |
|---|---|
| *rendre visite (à . . . )* | to pay a visit (to . . . ) |
| *une visite* | a visit |
| *s'amuser* | to enjoy onself, to have fun |
| *une / l'image* | a / the picture |
| *préféré, -e* | preferred, favorite |
| *fatigué, -e* | tired |
| *présenter* | to present, to introduce |
| *je te présente . . .* | Let me introduce . . . to you |
| *je voudrais* | I would like |
| *je comprends* | I understand |
| *je ne comprends pas* | I don't understand |
| *montrer* | to show |

| *et puis* | and then |
| *bien* | well |
| *mal* | poorly |
| *bientôt* | soon |
| *toujours* | always |
| *rarement* | scarcely, rarely |
| *quelquefois* | sometimes |
| *souvent* | often |
| *jamais* | never |
| *très* | very |
| *trop* | too |
| *tard* | late |
| *tôt* | early |
| *beaucoup (de . . .)* | a lot of (of . . .) |
| *assez (de . . .)* | enough (of . . .) |
| *un peu (de . . .)* | a little (of . . .) |
| *trop (de . . .)* | too much (of . . .) |
| *enfin* | finally / anyway |
| *pas du tout* | not at all |
| *avant* | before |
| *après* | after |

## PRACTICE EXERCISE 1

Fill in the blanks with the translation of the word or phrase given in English.

1. *Je ne travaille* (not at all) *le dimanche.*
2. *Alors, nous aimons* (to pay a visit) *à nos amis.*
3. *Je voudrais vous* (show) *une photo de nos* (daughters.)
4. *Ils font* (a little) *de sport.*
5. *L'hiver, il* (go) *au ski.*
6. *Et* (then) *en* (summer) *ils vont à la piscine toutes les semaines.*
7. *Ils aiment aussi faire* (often) *des promenades à la plage.*
8. *On s'amuse* (always) *avec eux !*

9. *Ah, c'est ma photo* (favorite).

10. *Je vous* (introduce) *mes amis et leur chien.*

---

**POINT 2:** ADVERBS

French adverbs are usually placed right after the verb. And just like their cousins in English, their forms never change. There's no masculine or feminine, singular or plural. How lucky!

—*Il chante très bien.*

—He sings very well.

—*Elle danse mal !*

—She dances poorly!

—*Je vais bientôt à Boston.*

—I am going to Boston soon.

—*Les enfants ont vraiment soif.*

—The children are really thirsty.

Adverbs are not just useful for telling how something is done, but also how often something is done. That gives us a spectrum of: *jamais, rarement, quelquefois, souvent, toujours . . .* (never, scarcely, sometimes, often, always . . .)

—*L'homme a toujours sommeil.*

—The man is always sleepy.

—*Vous allez souvent au stade.*

—You often go to the stadium.

—*Ma mère fait quelquefois du sport.*

—My mother plays sports sometimes.

—*Ils vont rarement au musée.*

—They rarely go to the museum.

They can also tell you to what extent something is done. So, we have: *pas du tout, un peu, assez, très, trop* . . . (not at all, a little, enough, very, too much . . .)

—*Nous avons très faim.*

—We are very hungry.

—*Son chien est trop joli.*

—Her / his dog is too cute.

—*Après la piscine, je suis un peu fatiguée.*

—After the swimming pool, I am a bit tired.


**PRACTICE EXERCISE 2**

Translate the adverbs in parentheses in order to complete the sentences.

1. *Il fait* (very) *froid.*

2. *Je vais à la maison parce que je suis* (really) *fatiguée.*

3. *Les étudiants vont* (rarely) *au théâtre.*

4. *Mes frères font* (often) *du ski.*

5. *Leur parents ne sont* (not at all) *sympas.*

6. *En Bretagne, on fait* (sometimes) *une promenade sur la plage.*

7. *Nous ne faisons* (never) *de balade en voiture.*

8. *Il fait* (too) *chaud pour travailler !*

9. *Ma famille va* (soon) *aller en voyage pour rendre visite à leurs amis.*

10. *Tu as des pommes ? Nos amis ont* (a little) *faim.*

11. *Elle n'aime pas manger très* (late).

12. *Ils vont à l'école* (very early).


**( WATCH THE DVD )**

This is just about the last time you'll be asked to do this, so if you're ready, watch Part 5, Section D, of your DVD. Then come back for one very last round of review exercises.

# *REVIEW EXERCISES*

### REVIEW EXERCISE 1

Translate the following sentences.

1. *Ils aiment rendre visite à leur parents.*
2. *Elle n'écoute jamais.*
3. *Son mari travaille beaucoup.*
4. *Ils vont souvent se promener en voiture.*
5. *Il fait un peu frais ce soir.*
6. *C'est une très belle photo de ma famille.*
7. *Parce qu'il pleut toujours, j'ai sommeil.*
8. *Quelquefois, nous allons au ski.*

### REVIEW EXERCISE 2

Rewrite the following sentences putting the words in the right order.

1. *vous /montrer/ Je / voudrais / cette / très / belle / photo.*
2. *en / allons / Nous / bientôt / France.*
3. *Je / faire / enchantée / vraiment / suis / votre / de / connaissance.*
4. *jamais / Ils / en / vont / été / ne / au / musée.*
5. *la / quelquefois / Ma / fait / vaisselle / sœur.*
6. *Tu / un peu / es / fatigué.*
7. *trop / Il / fait / pour / froid / une balade / faire.*
8. *On / pas du tout / n'aime / le football.*

### REVIEW EXERCISE 3

Write the opposites of these sentences.

1. *J'aime beaucoup les pommes.*
2. *Nous avons toujours froid.*
3. *Elles vont rarement au ciné.*
4. *Tu travailles trop.*
5. *Vous avez soif avant dîner.*

6. *Il fait très froid.*
7. *Les étudiants n'ont pas assez de vacances.*
8. *Nous allons toujours à la piscine.*

( **TAKE THE FINAL!** )

If you're ready for the comprehensive "final exam," go back to the DVD and see how you do!

# *Answer Key*

**PRACTICE EXERCISE 1**

**1.** pas du tout **2.** rendre visite **3.** montrer / filles **4.** un peu **5.** va **6.** puis / été **7.** souvent **8.** toujours **9.** préférée **10.** présente

**PRACTICE EXERCISE 2**

**1.** très **2.** vraiment **3.** rarement **4.** souvent **5.** pas du tout **6.** quelquefois **7.** jamais **8.** trop **9.** bientôt **10.** un peu **11.** tard **12.** très tôt

**REVIEW EXERCISE 1**

**1.** They like to visit their parents / pay a visit to their parents. **2.** She never listens. **3.** Her husband works a lot. **4.** They often go for a ride (in the car.) **5.** It's a bit chilly tonight. **6.** This is a very beautiful picture of my family. **7.** Because it's always raining, I'm sleepy. **8.** Sometimes, we go to ski.

**REVIEW EXERCISE 2**

**1.** Je voudrais vous montrer cette très belle photo. **2.** Nous allons bientôt en France. **3.** Je suis vraiment enchantée de faire votre connaissance. **4.** Ils ne vont jamais au musée en été. **5.** Ma sœur fait la vaisselle quelquefois. **6.** Tu es un peu fatigué. **7.** Il fait trop froid pour faire une balade. **8.** On n'aime pas du tout le football.

### REVIEW EXERCISE 3

**1.** Je n'aime pas beaucoup les pommes. **2.** Nous n'avons jamais froid. **3.** Elles vont souvent au ciné. **4.** Tu ne travailles pas assez. **5.** Vous avez soif après dîner. **6.** Il fait très chaud. **7.** Les étudiants ont trop de vacances. **8.** Nous n'allons jamais à la piscine.

# So, What's Next?
# Taking Your French Further

Now that you're off to a great start in French, you probably want to build on what you've learned. There are many ways that you can take your French further. If you're taking classes in school, well, keep doing that! And if you're not in school, there are probably courses that you can take in continuing education, at local community or cultural centers, or at private language schools. You could also practice what you know on the internet or by listening to the radio or watching French television. And, maybe now you can use your French to make a new friend.

No matter what you do, there are plenty of other fantastic Living Language® French programs available that will help you get the most out of any class. Or, you can use them entirely on their own. Go to *www.livinglanguage.com* for a complete online catalogue with full descriptions. You'll also find a few highlighted programs on the following pages.

*Bonne Chance, et Merci !*

# Notes

# Notes

# Notes

_____

_____

_____

_____

_____

_____

_____

_____

_____

_____

_____

_____

_____

_____

_____

_____